THE SILENT CRIME

What You Need

to Know

About

Identity Theft

Steffen Schmidt & Michael McCoy

Library of Congress Cataloging-in-Publication Data

The Silent Crime: What You Need to Know About Identity Theft by
Michael McCoy and Steffen W. Schmidt

Publisher : Twin Lakes Press
Editor: SEAS L.L.C.

Includes bibliographical references

ISBN: 978-0-9773260-1-3

1. Identity theft protection. 2. Consumer Education. 3. Data Security.
4. Hacking, phishing, personal information loss.

Back cover photograph of authors by:
Stan Brewer Photography
stanbrewer@mac.com

Identity Theft Prevention Institute Blog:
http://stolendata.blogspot.com/

National Information Protection Training and Certification Program
http://www.twinlakespress.com

Manufactured in the United States of America

10 9 8 7 6 5 4 3 2 1

For Lisa and Hoyt who put up with us during the frantic period of research for this book project.

I am very pleased to write the foreword to this outstanding new book on identity theft protection. In my many years as Attorney General of Mississippi and in my work in the field of law, I have seen the tragedy of identity theft up close.

Identity theft is a vicious crime that breaks the spirits of those who become victims. It unsettles their lives, costs them time and money, and in many cases leaves them frightened and worried that they will be forced to relive the nightmare in the future.

Stolen identities are also a major factor in such national policy issues as illegal immigration and terrorism. Many persons who are in the United States illegally use stolen or fabricated personal identities. In fact, federal law enforcement has been prosecuting illegals, using the crime of identity theft as a strong legal argument for raids, arrests, deportation, and jail. Most people will also remember that the September 11, 2001 terrorists all used false or stolen identities to plan and launch their attack against the United States.

In this book, Schmidt and McCoy present facts about identity theft in a clear and compelling way. Their illustrations of the types of identity theft are comprehensive. They remind us that these crimes can be committed close to home, even by family members or friends, and also from thousands of miles away by criminals who travel through cyberspace to snatch private information from computers and data banks.

The authors' use of real-life examples of crimes committed with false identities is important because it puts a tangible face on those who commit these crimes and what pain the victims go through in trying to prove THEIR innocence. These specific cases also make it easier for consumers to relate to this crime and see themselves as potential victims.

Finally, the authors' discussions of what consumers and institutions can do to reduce the risk of identity information loss and theft and how they can recover from such a loss is practical and helpful. In particular, Schmidt and McCoy review the many insurance and ID theft protection products that are available. They argue that these products can be very important for consumer peace of mind, knowing that someone is keeping an eye on credit ratings and other assets. ID theft protection services is also a helpful tool for recovering losses and using the legal assistance, law enforcement, and ultimately the justice system to restore the consumer's good name and credit, as well as catching and punishing those who commit these crimes.

The two authors bring to this project quite different personal backgrounds and experiences that help make this book exceptionally well rounded. Schmidt is a well-known professor at Iowa State University and a frequent commentator on national and international media. McCoy has 10 years in the insurance industry and is therefore familiar with the specific identity theft issues from that perspective. Both co-authored the sold out book on identity theft "Who is you? The Coming Epidemic of Identity Theft," on which this new work is based.

I highly recommend this book to consumers and the general public, but especially to professionals who work in law enforcement, the insurance industry, health professionals, government agencies at all levels, and other institutions or organizations that collect, hold, store, manage, or share private information. It is these stewards of identity information who are responsible and must in the end be held accountable for protecting this indispensable yet fragile personal asset.

-Mike Moore

About Mike Moore

Mike Moore was born in Pascagoula, Mississippi and attended the University of Mississippi Law School. Before becoming Attorney General of Mississippi in 1988, Moore was District Attorney in Pascagoula, Mississippi. He was named "Lawyer of the Year" by the National Law Journal in 1997.

Michael Moore filed the first state Medicaid lawsuit against the tobacco industry and traveled throughout the United States convincing other state attorneys general to also file suits. He was the primary negotiator in the deal and was the leader of the push for a national tobacco settlement. The settlement was ultimately for $246 billion to the states, including $4.1 billion for Mississippi. The film "The Insider" starring Al Pacino and Russell Crowe portrays some of the events leading up to this settlement. Moore appears in the film as himself in several scenes.

Moore is now head of an independent law practice, Mike Moore Law Firm LLC, located just outside Jackson, Mississippi. He also serves as the Chairman of the Board for the Partnership for a Healthy Mississippi, which is funded by money from the tobacco settlement. Moore also sits on the Board of Directors for the Campaign for Tobacco-Free Kids. Most recently Moore was involved in an effort to sue State Farm Insurance for its handling of policyholders' Hurricane Katrina claims. (Sun Herald, Wed, Jan. 23, 2008).

Sources:

PBS special; on the tobacco industry, http://www.pbs.org/wgbh/pages/frontline/shows/settlement/deal/people/moore.html

"Big Tobacco's Nemesis: Billions from a novel and untested legal strategy," Governing Magazine, http://governing.com/poy/1998/ptmoore.htm

Foreword

About Mike Moore

Preface

Introduction

Before we invite you to step into our latest book on identity theft and identity information risks, we want to share some general comments with you.

First, let's be clear that the loss of sensitive personal information and identity theft (which are not the same thing) is on an unprecedented rise. Both the volume and the variety of thefts, losses, and misuse of identities are accelerating. The San Diego based Identity Theft Resource Center reported a fourfold increase in personal information breaches in 2007. These included 162 million customer records compromised worldwide. That's equivalent to more than half the entire population of the United States. There was also the loss of data disks with the personal critical information of 25 million British citizens.

Second, we want you to understand clearly that YOU need to develop a sharp sense of privacy protection for any vital information about yourself. Practicing personal identity protection should become so ingrained in your day-to-day behavior that you handle it sub-consciously. In this book we share personal data loss stories so you can relate better to this problem. We also provide as much practical, concrete, and useful information as possible on how to secure your valuable identity assets. So that you can empathize better, we are sharing for the first time in this book the personal stories of real people who have been the victims of ID theft.

Third, you need to become an active citizen and constantly pester your local, state, and federal representatives so they will improve the laws and regulations on identity protection and on prosecutions for abuse of identity. The problem exists at all levels and we need to have law enforcement and the judiciary much more robust and aggressive. You also need to get your representatives in government to force government agencies to enact identity protection education and training programs. This is the most effective way of also making government agencies of every kind protect your and other people's sensitive, personal information. In this book we are also starting most chapters with a short summary of one criminal case in identity misuse. These are interesting and educational. At the end of the chapter we give you full details of that case in what we are calling "The Rest of the Case."

Fourth, we need YOU to join the army of advocates for more responsible business practices in managing sensitive data on customers. Some of the most atrocious cases of data and identity loss in the last few years have taken place within companies. This is unacceptable and, as consumers, we all must force businesses to tighten up their handling of our good names and information. Companies need to be pushed by their customers every day to be diligent and zealous in protecting the personal information of their clients. Too many of the unspeakable losses of information have occurred in businesses. In this book we cover some of those in more detail. The purpose is again to give you a clear idea of how these losses happen so you can be a more informed advocate for yourself, your family, and friends.

Fifth, and finally, we want to address the issue of whether purchasing identity theft protection for yourself and your family is a good idea or a waste of money. There have been several articles by journalists who, for one reason or another, tell consumers that they can monitor and take care of their credit and identity information on their own for little or no cost. This is true in theory. It is also true in theory that you can do a leg amputation on yourself. In 2007, Al Hill a 66-year old in California, who was cutting down a tree, amputated his own leg below the knee using only his pocketknife because the tree fell on him and his leg got caught under the tree. Just because something is possible does not mean it is the most desirable alternative.

The reality is that most people who have an identity theft don't have the time, patience, knowledge, or psychological fortitude to take care of their credit and identity information on their own. Consider these numbers from the Federal Trade Commission (FTC) the main federal agency dealing with these issues. It can take from 150 to 500 hours of your time and as much as $3,000 to fix the run-of-the-mill identity theft problem. More discouraging still is the fact that the FTC says that 41% of ID theft victims have not fully resolved the problem as many as two years after discovering the loss.

From all of our experience in both academia and the insurance business, we strongly recommend that people take out an appropriate policy. There are two compelling reasons to do so. First, this type of protection provides huge peace of mind. In effect, as we like to say, having ID theft protection is like putting smoke alarms in your home. Second, as the information above proves, it is a monumental and depressing task to try to do ID theft recovery as well as try to get charges filed and criminals who violate your privacy and security prosecuted. One identity theft service and policy even covers multiple aspects of ID theft protection as well as restoration, including access to legal counsel when it becomes necessary to secure a lawyer.

This book project is the result of the authors' conclusion that a second book on identity theft is sorely needed. We have been working on the second year of a National Science Foundation grant to research identity security issues and then develop informative material to train employees who handle sensitive information. Our work is also intended for the general public since consumers are the ones who in the end must make personal decisions about their identity information.

SEAS L.L.C. along with Twin Lakes Publishing, L.L.C. are partners in this current book project, both having a great track record of developing educational and training material. This includes Schmidt's work with his co-authors in writing the best selling American government college textbook "American Government and Politics Today," which first came out in 1984 and is now in 5 different editions with the hardback in its 19th edition. It also includes the first identity theft book by the authors. SEAS L.L.C. is also developing an Internet class that will be marketed nationally on how to conduct academic research, how to write a winning academic paper, and how to deliver professional oral presentations (face-to-face as well as virtual presentations on the Internet).

For this project we also approached Pre-Paid Legal Services (www.prepaidlegal.com), one of the oldest life events prepaid legal services companies in the United States. They have an extensive national identity theft educational and training program both for their sales force and also for consumers. They were excited about our proposal for a new book on ID theft and are partners in this project. We have been given access to lawyers who handle identity theft and to consumers who have suffered identity theft attacks. We are delighted to incorporate the insights from these in our current book because they provide the reader intimate and well-informed testimonials on ID theft. We want to thank the graphic design department for excellent work on the cover and manuscript design.

In addition, we need to make it clear that we do not endorse any particular ID insurance product or service. In this book we make reference to many of the identity theft products and plans that are on the market. Some, such as LifeLock, are very recent and there is as yet no track record of success or failure to report, while others, such as Pre Paid Legal Services Inc. has been in business for over thirty years, and has partnered with Kroll Worldwide to offer the Identity Theft Shield[SM].

We feel that people must select a plan from the many choices that fits both their needs and budget. We do disagree fundamentally with the idea that a proactive service or insurance is not necessary because people can do it themselves. No consumers want first to learn what to do when their credit, medical records or other identity is breached and then spend 50 to 500 hours and thousands of dollars, not to mention endless sleepless nights worrying, to recover their losses. Most people would gladly purchase ID theft protection just for the peace of mind.

We want to thank the many colleagues and former information assurance students who have written essays for this book. These are valuable contributions to understanding identity theft.

Before we move on into the first chapter of the book, we the authors would like to introduce ourselves.

Michael McCoy has spent over 10 years in the insurance industry and therefore has a long history of understanding the pain of clients hit by personal information or identity losses. He also has seen the relief in customers and acquaintances when their ID protection plan kicked in and either avoided a serious ID theft or helped to efficiently and relatively painlessly restore and reset everything to normal. McCoy is also an instructor at Des Moines Area Community College, teaching state, national, and international political policy.

McCoy is the lead researcher for the Center for Information Protection (CIP) National Science Foundation (NSF) Identity Theft Prevention and Protection Education Project at Iowa State University. This project involves the development of new and highly effective training for persons working with sensitive information in government, academia, non-profits and the private sector. McCoy is a leader in developing identity theft educational material as well as providing seminars and lectures throughout North America. He is a frequent and much sought-out lecturer throughout the United States on identity theft and sensitive information loss. He developed and is working with others on a national critical information and ID theft certification program for state insurance and other personnel. This certification was field tested in 2007 in an on-line, asynchronous Internet format and will soon be released nationally.

Co-author Dr. Steffen Schmidt has done university research and teaching for 39 years at Long Island University,

Southampton College and at Iowa State University. He is also an associate of the Nova Southeastern University in Ft Lauderdale, Florida. He is the principal investigator (PI) for a National Science Foundation (NSF) project on identity theft education and prevention, which is now in its second year of funding. This NSF project is extracting insights from behavioral and policy research to create an efficient employee identity theft training program for the insurance industry and law enforcement. Schmidt is also a member of the faculty of the Information Assurance graduate program at Iowa State University, which educates students in hardware, software, educational, and policy aspects of ID theft protection. He is an internationally recognized lecturer, who has been quoted by many print and electronic media, has been on CNN, the BBC, Canadian Television, NPR, CNN in Spanish, (Schmidt is fluent in several languages), and many other news media. He has a weekly public radio show on WOI radio, where he is known as Dr. Politics, and appears every week on the talk radio show Chowder in the Morning with host Arnie Arneson on 1110 WCCM, New Hampshire. He is the lead author of the best selling college textbook in American Government published by Wadsworth Publishing, has written eleven other books and close to 150 technical, scholarly, and professional articles.

Both Schmidt and McCoy are regular contributing writers on the popular Identity Theft Prevention Institute blog, ***www.stolendata.blogspot.com.***

Q. What is Identity Theft?

A. " Identity theft occurs when someone possesses or uses your name, address, Social Security number, bank or credit card number, or other identifying information without your knowledge with the intent to commit fraud or other crimes" (FTC)

Q. Why should I monitor my credit report on a regular basis?

A. In many cases this will be your only way to learn of suspicious activity. It will be your early warning detector that someone else is using your good name and credit for their financial gain.

Q. What do I do when I become a victim of identity theft?

A. Pray! Unless you have immediate access to an attorney and a service that monitors your credit and restores it when you become a victim.

Q: Why do they need all the information on the order form?

A: They need the information to verify your identity. Advanced security screens make sure that your request is valid and that you are who you say you are.

Q: Won't signing up for a credit monitoring service hurt my credit?

A: No. Consumers have the right to look at their credit report without it affecting their credit or credit score. When you request your credit report it's called a "consumer pull" and has no affect on your credit. Only when you ask a possible creditor to inquire about your credit can it affect your score.

"Blissful Ignorance" About Identity Theft?

Dhananjay Nayakankuppam, an assistant professor of marketing at the University of Iowa, and his team have done research on whether the amount of information consumers have about a product influences how optimistic they feel about that product. Prof. Nayakankuppam discovered that people who have only a little information about a product are happier with their purchases than people who have more information. They decided to call this phenomenon "The Blissful Ignorance Effect." *(The Des Moines Register, February 1, 2008).*

We found this to be fascinating because it dovetails so perfectly with our extensive qualitative research over the past four years in the area of social behavior and identity theft. The evidence from public as well as in-house studies, to which we have had access, suggests that consumers would rather ignore risk and go on with life than fret and worry about potential identity theft. In other words, most people would rather exhibit "blissful ignorance" regarding identity theft loss than proceed with the confusing, complex, time consuming, and expensive process of securing and protecting their identity.

Prof. Nayakankuppam indicated, "The less you know about a product, the easier it is to engage in wishful thinking. The more information you have, the harder it is to kid yourself." This is paralleled by the findings from our review of the literature on identity theft that suggests that the more information about ID theft people have, the more worried and unhappy they are about the security of that information. The less information consumers or employees handling sensitive data have, the more confident they are that the data is secure. Conversely, as with Nayakankuppam's research, our studies indicate that the more information people have about identity theft, the more convinced they are that the data is vulnerable and the higher their level of anxiety.

One of the cases we studied involved a professional woman, let's call her Maricelle, who had traveled for several weeks in Asia on business for her boutique clothing store. On her return she discovered that she had left her Palm Pilot in the pocket in front of her airline seat. The airline "Lost and Found" had no reports of the device.

We received a call from Maricelle asking whether she should do something about this lost device because in addition to her business appointments, birthdays, anniversaries and other information, she kept all of her credit card, checking account, PayPal, Amazon and other login passwords and bank PIN numbers in that device.

Her reaction was to engage in "Blissful Ignorance" or "Irrational naiveté" by suppressing her feelings that all this information might be at risk, instead saying things like, "No one who finds it will really want all that information, right?" and "They will delete everything and sell it to someone, I'm pretty sure?"

When we dug a little deeper, we began to uncover the real fear and anxiety related to the difficulty in trying to secure all of this information. "Is there someplace I can call that will take care of all this?" was a telling question.

We were very sympathetic. Think about all the web sites, credit cards, and other "accounts" you have that require you to log in with a user name and a password or PIN. Do you even know all the accounts and sites where you have registered and which would be in that Palm Pilot or address book? If not, imagine the nightmare of trying to make an accurate list of all these accounts after you lose the device with your list and then going to these accounts (without the benefit of the list that you left on the airplane) and changing critical information such as passwords?!

Under those circumstances it is easier psychologically to go into denial and convince yourself that YOUR loss of critical information is not that likely to lead to any serious consequences. After all, it is easier to do that and hope (or even pray) that nothing will happen than to try to remember all the accounts you have and fix them.

In the field of public policy and political behavior, there is a similar phenomenon that has been studied for many years called the "Rational Ignorance Effect." How can ignorance be rational you ask? Rational Ignorance is part of economic theory and related to calculus. Here is what Robert Schenk writes about this effect on his web site (http://ingrimayne.com/econ/LogicOfChoice/RatIgnorance.html):

"The amount of time people spend obtaining information differs from product to product. They will spend less time learning about the bicycle they give their child than they will learning about a new car. The larger the purchase, the larger the potential benefit of a few hours spent learning about the purchase."

One of the problems with personal identity information is that people do not view it as a product. They have come to see their Social Security numbers, credit cards and bank passwords as rights, not as commodities. Therefore, people do not assign a value to this information. Without a cash value, they see very little reason to invest even a small amount of time in understanding and protecting that information.

"The government has many policies that involve major sums of money. For example, a major weapons system in the defense department can cost $50 billion. This amounts to about $200 for every person in the United States, or $1000 for a family of five. Yet few people spend much time studying these policies. A reason is that to understand them requires many hours of study, and the probability that an understanding of them will change them in any way is very small. Thus, for most citizens the benefit of learning about a program that does not directly affect them is small, the cost is large, and they end up not knowing much about the program. Economists say that these poorly informed citizens are rationally ignorant."

Once again this pertains to identity protection. For most people everything that happens on the back end of their activities such as charging with credit cards or logging into PayPal is incomprehensively complex. When you swipe your credit card, or nowadays with some of the new radio frequency cards, wave it in front of a scanner, what happens after that? How is the information read? Where is it sent? How is it managed once received by the company? Where is it stored? With whom is that information shared? Is it managed in a form that only authorized people can access and read?

Almost NO consumer wants to invest time in learning all of that. Moreover, we have found in our research that when people start thinking about it, they begin to experience anxiety because they realize that this is all probably very sloppy and that there are risks. If they continued to think this way, they would need to make a decision and stop using credit cards, on-line accounts, and so forth, which is almost impossible in 21st century modern societies. Thus, most consumers swipe their cards or store their account passwords on their phones or in little booklets in their purses and "rationally ignore" all these anxiety-inducing thoughts.

Schenk continues, *"There is vastly more to know than any one person can possibly know. To survive and prosper in the world, one must seek that knowledge which will benefit the seeker. Most people would consider someone a bit odd who was not planning to buy a car, but went from dealer to dealer trying to learn all he could about relative car prices in the name of intellectual curiosity. The behavior of most citizens suggests that they also consider odd the seeking of in-depth knowledge about the pros and cons of a specific government policy if that knowledge does not directly benefit the person who gets it. The hypothesis of the rationally ignorant voter suggests that people will be better informed about the choices they make in the marketplace than about those they make in the voting booth."*

The "rational consumer" therefore generally ignores exposure to any of the many ways that his or her identity information could be put at risk and continues going about his or her business. In fact, this behavior is at the root of identity theft loss both by consumers and by personnel managing such information on behalf of students, patients, employees, or customers.

Maricelle, our acquaintance who lost her Palm Pilot, asked one of the most compelling questions we've heard from persons on the edge of identity theft when she wanted to know if there was any overarching and low hassle solution to fixing sensitive data loss. "Do you have a magic way to take care of this problem?" she queried. We told her that there are some pretty good services that can help by monitoring accounts; then, if unauthorized or criminal activity is detected, by informing credit card companies, the bank, and other sensitive places - changing the locks on the door so to speak.

To our surprise she then said, "No, I mean a magic solution to all the different passwords and PIN numbers and other stuff we have to use even to update our software on the computer? I can never remember those, so I have to write them down."

We have in fact been working with a bunch of computer and data mining geeks to invent such a solution. It would basically involve a device the size of an Apple iTouch™ into which the consumers enter their accounts, PIN numbers, addresses, sensitive phone numbers, and other data. The device would convert all that information into highly encrypted files at the National Security Agency *Advanced Encryption Standard (AES)*, Rijndae level. (Don't ask. This is an encryption standard developed by two Belgian cryptographers, Joan Daemen and Vincent Rijmen, which is very effective, relatively easy to implement, and requires little memory.)

The consumer would only need to remember his or her login and password to this device *(we call it The Internet Safe)*. The device would open when the legitimate owner asked it to do so. Once the password was entered, the device would decrypt the stored information. The owner could use it to, say, log into PayPal, and then when the owner logged out, the device would lock up. No one could get any of this information without the requisite security information. The consumer would only need to remember *one login and one password!*

The Internet Safe would be a futuristic but reasonable technological fix to what we call the "Crisis of Passwords." For a few hundred dollars it could be a solution almost any consumer would prefer over "Blissful Ignorance."

Even this device would NOT fix all of the other data losses that consumers endure. It would not protect people from the intruders who break into mailboxes around the first of February and remove the IRS W-2, 1099 forms, and a host of other forms reporting people's incomes. Those forms all have Social Security numbers written on them and are the easiest of pickings. This device also would not be able to get around the irrational neglect of risk demonstrated by the guy at the gym who left his wallet in the unprotected locker.

If we understand the pervasiveness of "rational ignorance" as well as the clear existence of the "Blissful Ignorance Effect" described by professor Nayakankuppam, we can understand why identity theft is growing at such a furious pace.We can also make a much better case why most people would be wise to sign up for some insurance or identity monitoring service because most people are in deep denial about the risks and they would rather ignore them for temporary peace of mind than take the time even to put combination locks on their gym lockers!

This book is premised on the insights into human risk behavior that we discussed above. These fundamental behavioral characteristics, which we are studying in greater depth with a National Science Foundation grant and our work with the Iowa State University Center for Information Protection (CIP), are vitally important to understanding the remainder of this book. These insights are also the reason why one of the key long term solutions to critical information loss is to train people to change their behavior by making it clear that identity information has a price, that it is a very valuable and expensive product, and that consumers and employees need to treat it as such.

The table below depicts the two paths for consumers and employees handling sensitive identity information. The top path follows the "Blissful Ignorance" effect that will lead to greater risk of ID information loss. The second, lower path, leads to greater ID security.

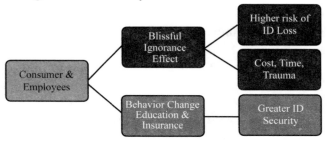

Let us briefly look at the issue of children and ID theft, which is a classic example of blissful ignorance about a very important part of ID theft.

Children and Identity Theft
Co-written by: Susan Kerr – Fraud Investigator Iowa Attorney Generals Office

"Identity theft and the theft of our personal information is out of control," Clinton says in a written statement. "No one is safe, not even kids and young adults, as identity thieves carry out electronic muggings that can cost people cash and their credit records."

—Sen. Hillary Rodham Clinton, D-N.Y.

As we have traveled across North America lecturing and giving seminars on identity theft, one of the most common questions we receive is "How do I protect my children's identity or monitor their credit files?" The theft of your child's identity should be a terrifying thought. Minors are perfect targets for identity theft, as they have clean credit histories and thieves can get away with the crime for years because parents rarely check the credit reports of their children. The New York State Consumer Protection Board reported to the Federal Trade Commission in March 2007 that "it was witnessing an increase in unauthorized use of children's identifying information…"

"Children's identities are stolen and then used to obtain credit cards, get driver's licenses or open accounts. Often, the information is sold for use by illegal immigrants or individuals attempting to restart their lives and avoid arrest. "One advantage from a criminal standpoint: The crime may not be discovered for a long period of time." Linda Foley, founder of the Identity Theft Resource Center, said the problem is that a credit issuer must try to authenticate who that person is and depending on the situation, it's difficult to authenticate who that person is."

—————————*http://www.wesh.com/money/15121374/detail.html*

More disturbing is the fact that many parents with poor credit ratings use their children's identity and Social Security number, which then is burdened with bad credit or other misuse. Once the child turns 18 and wants to obtain credit, a credit card or some other instruments, the child discovers that his/her name and identity has been ruined for many years.

Consumer advocates attribute the escalation to the early

issuing of Social Security numbers and the overuse of these numbers. For example parents who want to claim their child for a tax deduction are required to have a Social Security number for a child older than one. They can get the number for a newborn child by applying at a Social Security office, by mail or they can obtain the child's number by the Enumeration at Birth program which began in 1989 and lets parents fill out the information at the hospital before taking the baby home.

Kids have to provide their Social Security numbers as proof of identity for schools, medical services, insurance companies, financial institutions, and cell phone providers and there is no federal law that prohibits an organization or a company from asking for a Social Security number.

Since your child is issued a Social Security number in most cases before his/her first birthday and that number is used throughout their lifetime, it is important to begin by limiting where you and your child leave that number. A Social Security number is the key that unlocks much of your identity. Whenever possible, use an alternative form of identification, such as; student identification number, driver's license number, or a random issued number from the entity you are dealing with.

When sharing personal identifying information at the doctor's office, on the Internet, on the phone, at the cash register or enrolling at school, ask key questions such as;

- *Will my information be shared with affiliates or third parties?*
- *What safeguards are in place to protect my information?*
- *How will my information be stored and eventually disposed of?*

Generally speaking, minors should not have credit reports or data compiled in their names by the credit repositories, but in some instances this does occur. Recently, I have asked this question concerning my own child and subsequently created a file on her behalf. I started by sending in a free "annual credit report request form" to Experian. I chose to contact only one of three credit report providers, with the intention of getting in touch with the other two companies later in the year. In about one week's time I received the following response, addressed to my child, stating:

Dear --------------,

We are responding to your request for a free annual credit report. We were unable to locate credit information about you because either you did not provide sufficient identification information for us to verify your identity, or you have not established a credit history. If you would like us to recheck our records, please send us all of the following information: ...
Sincerely,

Experian
NCAC
P.O. Box 9702
Allen, TX 75013

The above letter does not mean that my daughter has absolutely not been a victim of identity theft. However, it assures me that (at least as far as Experian has investigated) no one has opened up, asked for, or obtained credit in her name – a small victory for our household. To further investigate possible violations of my daughter's financial identity, I would request the free inquiries from the other two major credit repositories to confirm my previous findings.

Concerning the monitoring of a minor's financial identity, we recommend that you have your child's credit report checked annually, or at the very least when the child is 16 or 17 years of age. You can check this information free of charge once every year with annualcreditreport.com, the only official government-sanctioned website for such matters. This plan provides you with immediate peace of mind, and checking her credit report before your child turns 18 will allow you time to rectify any discrepancies before she becomes a legal adult. You should use the aforementioned website to monitor your own personal information as well.

Many of our children, grandchildren, nieces and nephews are surfing the web. Whether it is playing games, shopping, or studying, today's kids are drawn to the Internet. But when it comes to them sharing their personal information online, who's in charge? The Federal Trade Commission has established new rules for website owners to make sure that our kids' privacy is protected while they're online. These rules are part of the 1998 Children's Online Privacy Protection Act (COPPA).

Remember, Identity thieves also use children's Social Security numbers to falsely obtain jobs, avoid filing taxes or obtain government benefits. Request a copy of your child's earnings statement from the Social Security Administration by calling 800-772-1213 or online at www.ssa.gov/mystatement.

Let us now take a closer look in Chapter 1 at the specific details of personal information, personal identity proof, andthe accelerating threat to personal security posed by these.the accelerating threat to personal security posed by these.

CHAPTER 1

THE CRISIS OF IDENTITY THEFT

"R. Alexander Acosta, United States Attorney for the Southern District of Florida, and Jonathan I.

Solomon, Special Agent in Charge, Federal Bureau of Investigation announced that two (2) defendants who were convicted of conspiracy, identity theft, computer fraud and wrongful disclosure of individually identifiable health information (HIPAA violation) were sentenced by United States District Court Judge James I. Cohn, on Friday, April 27, 2007."

"The Rest of The Case" is at the end of this chapter.

As we completed our book Who is You? *The Coming Epidemic of Identity Theft* several years ago the following news story had just broken:

"This June, when news broke that 40 million Master

Cards had been hacked, was one of the most discouraging days in recent memory. It's not just that we would now all have to carefully scrutinize our credit card statements, which we hate to do – who saves all those receipts from charges at bars, car rentals, latte shops! It was also the first time that we realized our life is a seamless appendage of our Social Security number and our credit cards."

We did not know at that time that things would go steeply downhill from there. Most of what was being written two years ago said, "Everything is under control. Don't worry. Move on. All is being taken care of. The government will come to the rescue" or something to that effect.

How wrong they were!

Time Magazine wrote in its first January, 2008 issue,

"162 million"

"Number of personal-data records affected in security breaches reported by 302 organizations in 2007"

One Hundred and sixty two million is an astonishingly large number given that the US population is 303,220,825 million at the time we are writing this book according to the US population clock. *http://www.census.gov/main/www/popclock.html*

The week of the big MasterCard credit card hack in 2005, Steffen Schmidt wrote:

"That week I was on my way to New York for some meetings and research on identity theft that included a trip to the United Nations.

I checked in at the airport by sliding my credit card through the swipe at the check- in kiosk and my travel record promptly popped up on the screen.

*"Yikes" I thought, "**I am** my credit card!" The airline will release my boarding pass, let me change seat assignments, and generally talk to the airline with the simple reading of my credit card! Truth be told, that magnetic strip on the back of my card (and yours as well) has a lot more information than just a credit card number. Most people don't know this and the companies are reluctant to spill the beans, but those little strips contain part of your life history.*

But I digress.

What if my credit card had been hacked, stolen and I could not get my boarding pass at the kiosk? No problem, you can still check in with your reservation number, or your flight number and your ID at the counter (but not at the kiosk).

Having successfully made it through check in, security, and onto the plane, I suddenly thought "What if my card has been hacked and cancelled – I show up at the front desk of my toney downtown Manhattan hotel and the fruffy clerk says "Ahhh ... mmm, sir, I'm sorry, but I need to impound your card. It shows up as stolen. Do you have another credit card? ... and ... may I see your identification please."

"Of course I have a Visa, Master Card, American Express," I thought as I mulled over this hypothetical scenario, "so I'll just use one of the others."

Then I realized that the story about the 40 million hacked cards went on to say (I saw this on CNN) that many different types of credit cards were processed at the contractor that was hacked and that they did not know but thought others besides Master Card had been stolen. In my increasingly panicked state of self-induced anxiety I could see myself in

New York City with no credit, no way to check into the hotel, no way to buy a meal, get a cab ride, hit a bar and order a double Manhattan ... in other words, no way to survive.

Nowadays who carries cash like my dad used to do in those days before plastic.

Obviously my identity, "Who is me?" is to a significant extent defined by the digital information on my credit card and my reputation and behavior that entitles me to use the card as a surrogate for money. Imagine! I can't rent a car without a credit card even if I have a wad of $1,000 bills in my pocket, as a hapless Colombian drug lord found out at Miami International.

Credit card theft is only one of the spokes on the wheel of identity theft, but it is a crucial one in early twenty first century America. However, it is only one of the spokes on the wheel of my identity. Obviously had someone stolen my entire identity – my name, my birth date, my social security number, my medical history, my educational records, my employment history – things would be infinitely worse."

Of course, data loss does not necessarily mean identity theft but it is the precursor, a necessary condition, for the worst to happen. In some cases stolen identities are used by people to engage in financial crime, fraud, child pornography, to become illegal immigrants in the US, to get false educational or medical records, and perhaps even to commit acts of terrorism.

"... morally flexible miscreants committing identity theft both on and off the Web, lined their pockets with nearly $50 billion in ill-gotten gains in [2004], according to the Federal Trade Commission. As if that's not bad enough, the FTC says U.S. consumers reported losses from fraud of more

than $400 million last year. And ... increasingly, the weapon of choice is the Internet." "Stolen Names, Big Numbers," <u>American Demographics</u>, Sept 1, 2004 by David Myron

As it turns out the Internet is NOT the biggest of your worries and the amounts cited above were peanuts.

Consider this news from the end of 2007.

"London, 11/20/2007. *The British government today revealed it has lost the private and sensitive data of 25 million of its citizens, reports BBC.com [1].*

Two computer discs holding the personal details of all families in the UK with a child under 16 have gone missing. The Child Benefit data on them includes name, address, date of birth, National Insurance number and, where relevant, bank details of 25m people. Chancellor Alistair Darling said there was no evidence the data had gone to criminals - but urged people to monitor bank accounts "for unusual activity."

In an emergency statement before Members of Parliament (MPs), Darling said the data breach occurred when junior officials at HM Revenue and Customs (HMRC), which is responsible for paying children's benefits, failed to observe security protocols when sending two computer discs by mail to the National Audit Office.

The discs, according to records, never arrived."

Security Management
—*http://www.securitymanagement.com/print/2821*

This data loss did not happen in cyberspace and it could NOT have been prevented by the individual citizens who had their identities lost. It was some incompetent bureaucrats who failed their citizens. That amounted to 40% of all

Brits; yes, you read that correctly, 25 million people = about 40%.

The frightening thing is that you are really nobody except a piece of plastic lamination; a number, and maybe a picture.

In fact, as we have indicated in our training seminars and lectures, for most Americans **the driver's license is them!**

In 2008, the US Congress is debating how to make this document more fool proof and secure. In fact, Congress really wants to create a national standard for drivers' licenses that must be used by all states. That, of course, raises a whole other problem, which is the question of whether this then becomes more or less a "National ID Card." There are pluses and minuses to a national identity document. We will discuss this issue in another chapter.

When you show that laminated license to the airline agent at the check-in counter and to the security checker as you prepare to enter the frequent-flier torture of the metal detector, "… Take off your shoes! Laptop out of the briefcase! Remove your coats please! Keys and change in this plastic bowl!" Walk through the TSA line; they have no independent way of determining if you, is really you. After all, your picture does not even look like you!

There is no fingerprint, DNA, or retinal scan. In fact there is very little with which to double check the validity of your identity.

If someone has successfully seized all of your information, say through an Internet hack, and has been issued a driver's license, a passport and other identification, then he/she can obtain credit cards as you, can buy real estate as you, can marry as you, and engage in contracts as you. And, they can enter airports and fly on airplanes **as you.**

It becomes a serious problem for you if they've been identified as engaging in criminal behavior, there is a warrant out for them, or they are suspected terrorists. In this case, when you show your ID, you can be arrested as them! If their name was given to the Homeland Security Department and you are on a watch list, you will be arrested when you enter security or try to check in at the ticket counter (even though you are not who they are really after). Or you may be pried off a plane in Paris or Hong Kong because your name is on the list! You know that you are not this person, but you have almost no way of proving it because **this person has become you.**

Schmidt also wrote in his journal:

When I successfully got to New York, ... checked into my hotel with my credit card, and proceeded with my meetings, I realized how incredibly vulnerable we all are to a coming epidemic of identity theft.

I also realized how disastrous this epidemic will be for us not only as individuals but also for the stability and continuity of our country. For, not only is identity theft a crime against our personal integrity, if left unchecked and unpunished, it will also profoundly affect our economy, the way we travel and live, and the very security of our nation, which is already threatened by terrorists and "evil doers."

Credit card companies have been keen on developing fraud prevention tools and the most effective to date has apparently been the placing of a special three code number on the back of the card, on the strip where you sign your name. This information is supposedly not kept in records with the card and is only **on the card itself**. Thus, someone cannot simply get hold of your credit card number and then abuse it. They actually also have to have the verification number in order to make charges on the Internet or on the phone. We ask ourselves, "If the three identity numbers are not kept anywhere except on the card then how does Amazon.com, or e-bay know that they are the correct numbers?" How do they verify that these are right? The numbers are stored on the credit card server and maybe even on individual store verification systems.

These are the little discrepancies in the whole information security hype and spin that we would like to explore in this book.

We think of this book is a **self-defense manual on identity and financial theft.**

Our objective is to train **you** in the "karate" of identity defense.

One of the things we are stressing more in this new book is the availability of passive security protection that people can purchase. This ranges from programs that pay you some cash to do a recovery program by hiring a professional to programs that monitor your credit and finance 24-7 to policies that actually secure legal assistance before, during, and after an identity theft incident by providing around-the-clock legal access. We suggest that consumers use a combination of personal identity protection and paid services that best fit their needs.

It is also our goal to have you become incensed at the incredible irresponsibility of corporations, schools, colleges, hospitals, pharmacies, loan companies, and the bureaucracy, all of which have failed and failed miserably to safeguard your precious personal information.

If this book results in numerous class action law suits by persons who have suffered the trauma, pain, and terrible loss of personal identity, we will have achieved one of our goals.

Something needs to be done and done urgently to secure

our "me"; our precious personal identity. If you read the full case study of medical identity theft at the end of this chapter you will see how seriously this could affect you or family members and friends.

We are your allies in this battle.

Oh, by the way, Time Magazine, January of 2008 also reported the following statistic:

"19"

"The number of these [162 million in 2007] security-breach cases in which arrests or prosecutions have been made."

The Rest of the Case

Southern District of Florida - Press Release http://www.usdoj.gov/usao/fls/PressReleases/070503-01.html
1 of 1 1/16/08 7:06 AM
The United States Attorney's Office
Southern District of Florida
Press Release
TWO DEFENDANTS SENTENCED IN HEALTH CARE FRAUD, HIPAA, AND
IDENTITY THEFT CONSPIRACY
May 3, 2007
FOR IMMEDIATE RELEASE
R. Alexander Acosta, United States Attorney for th
Southern District of Florida, and Jonathan I.

Solomon, Special Agent in Charge, Federal Bureau of Investigation announced that two (2) defendants who were convicted of conspiracy, identity theft, computer fraud and wrongful disclosure of individually identifiable health information (HIPAA violation) were sentenced by United States District Court Judge James I. Cohn, on Friday, April 27, 2007. Fernando Ferrer, Jr. and Isis Machado were convicted of conspiracy to commit computer fraud, conspiracy to commit identity theft and conspiracy to wrongfully disclose individually identifiable health information, in violation of 18 U.S.C. § 371.

Ferrer was also convicted of a substantive count of fraud in connection with computers in violation of 18 U.S.C. § 1030, a substantive count of violating the Health Insurance Portability and Accountability Act (HIPAA) involving the wrongful disclosure of individually identifiable health information, in violation of 42 U.S.C § 1320d-6(a)(2), and five separate counts of aggravated identity theft, in violation 18 U.S.C. § 1028A. Ferrer pled not guilty and proceeded to trial. He was convicted by a jury of all 8 counts of the Superseding Indictment. Machado pled guilty to conspiracy and testified at trial against Ferrer.

Defendant Machado was employed at the Cleveland Clinic. Machado and her cousin Ferrer, obtained the personal information of Cleveland Clinic and Health Management Associates (HMA) patients, including, among other information, the patients' names, dates of birth, Social Security numbers, Medicare numbers, and addresses, and used the patients' information to make fraudulent claims for Medicare reimbursement upon the United States, allegedly on behalf of more than 1,100 victims and in an amount in excess of $2.5 million. Ferrer advised Machado of an "opportunity" whereby Machado could sell stolen personal identification information to her co-conspirators. Machado exceeded her authorized access to the Cleveland Clinic's computer system to obtain and print out personal information of Cleveland Clinic and HMA patients. Machado then provided this personal information to Ferrer in return for payment. Ferrer then caused the personal information obtained by Machado to be used to file fraudulent claims for Medicare reimbursement upon the United States. Cleveland Clinic reported the allegations to the FBI, which began the investigation as a result of the information provided by Cleveland Clinic.

Ferrer was sentenced to 87 months in prison, 3 years of supervised release, and ordered to pay restitution in the amount of $2,505,883.43. Machado was sentenced to 3 years probation, including 6 months of home confinement, and also ordered to pay restitution in the amount of $2,505,883.43.

This case is a sobering example of how vulnerable we are to criminal intrusion into our private records. It is all the more frightening to see medical records abused since any mistakes resulting from unauthorized activities with these could result in dangerous and even deadly results for the real patient (such as wrong medication or procedures prescribed as a result of someone else's treatment being commingled with that of the legitimate patient).

Now that we have reviewed the basics of identity and identity information loss, let's take a quick tour of the actual parameters of personal identity. A little trip through history is always informative and helps better put into perspective the analysis that follows.

CHAPTER 2

HISTORY

"I don't have any personal history," he said after a long pause. "One day I found out that personal history was no longer necessary for me and, like drinking, I dropped it." ... from Carlos Castaneda, Journey To Ixtlan

It would be nice to erase our personal history. Then no one could steal our identity, which is really all of the accumulated personal history of ourselves including all the dates (birth, school graduation, job dates, surgery, car accident, etc.) and all those numbers (Social Security, bank account, selective service, credit card) that we all accumulate over a lifetime.

Tim Boucher provides a long excerpt from Castaneda, which we believe is worth reading.

I don't have any personal history," he said after a long pause. "One day I found out that personal history was no longer necessary for me and, like drinking, I dropped it." ...

I stared at him, trying to detect the hidden meanings of his words.

"How can one drop one's personal history?" I asked in an argumentative mood.

"One must first have the desire to drop it," he said. "And then one must proceed harmoniously to chop it off, little by little." …

"You don't know what I am, do you?" he said as if he were reading my thoughts. "You will never know, who or what I am, because I don't have a personal history." …

Don Juan said that everybody that knew me had an idea about me, and that I kept feeding the idea with everything I did. "Don't you see?" he asked dramatically. "You must renew your personal history by telling your parents, your relatives, and your friends everything you do. On the other hand, if you have no personal history, no explanations are needed; nobody is angry or disillusioned with your acts. And above all no one pins you down with their thoughts." …

"It is best to erase all personal history," he said slowly, as if giving me time to write it down in my clumsy way, "because that would make us free from the encumbering thoughts of other people." …

"Little by little you must create a fog around yourself; you must erase everything around you until nothing can be taken for granted, until nothing is any longer for sure, or real. Your problem now is that you're too real. Your endeavors are too real; your moods are too real. Don't take things so for granted. You must begin to erase yourself." … http://www.timboucher.com/journal/2006/12/09/erasing-personal-history/

Since this is a book about identity theft, we don't want to get sucked into the "Toltec" culture that Mr. Castaneda analyzed, popularized, and which now has many followers. But, we think it is interesting to remember that we are vulnerable to identity theft precisely because we HAVE personal identities – the "Me" – and it is all of the accumulated historical events, numbers, and stories of us that become vulnerable to theft and misuse.

There is also advice in books and several web sites not necessarily related to Mr. Castaneda, on how to erase your personal history. One list includes the following steps:

1. *Get rid of old photos and memorabilia. They keep you rooted in the past.*
2. *Change your name and address often, if possible.*
3. *Stop using the words "I," "me," and "myself" as much as possible. This will free up your awareness.*
4. *Stop talking about your past, age, culture, degrees, job, titles, etc.*
5. *Change your appearance periodically (hair, clothes, etc.). This deters having a fixed self-image.*
6. *Stop having pictures taken of you.*
7. *Avoid getting too enmeshed with other people. Keep your relationships fluid and open.*
8. *Stop explaining all your comings and goings to others.*

http://www.lightworks.com/monthlyAspectarian/2004/March/feature2.htm

Again, we are sharing this information with you to raise YOUR awareness of what constitutes the YOU that becomes vulnerable to id theft. If you look at the list above, you will begin to recognize that you should probably exercise care when giving out too much information to people or organizations. You should certainly change your passwords and maybe even your credit cards frequently.

As a sidebar, criminals and those who do not want to be detected by the authorities also want to erase their personal histories and replace them with fictitious ones, perhaps even yours! There are many books written about how to "change" who you are and generally this is not seen by society and the authorities as some interesting literary or anthropological choice but as a potential first step in hiding illegal behavior. For example the web site http://www.ariza-research.com/new-id/ says:

Discover the Insider Secrets of Identity Changing

We live in complicated times. Fact is, the only way to walk away from your past problems is to change your identity. Though changing your identity may sound like a drastic step, today more and more people are doing it.

Why? Because the only really effective way to get a second chance at life is to create a new identity in an entirely new name - supported by a full set of genuine identity documents. Only then can you forget your old problems and at the same time guarantee your future freedom.

However, we have always lived in a world where the authorities and others expected to know who we are. Therefore, people have stolen others' identities throughout all of history.

As we said earlier the authorities no doubt carefully monitor this web site since it suggests the possibility of identity changes for criminal purposes. Either that or it could be an identity theft site in itself.

As a reminder, societies have looked for ways to verify who someone is since earliest times.

There are records of ancient Chinese clay fingerprint tablets that were used to tell one important person apart from another. Of course, common people were mostly irrelevant to the authorities. But, even among commoners (especially at the village level) people were known and recognized and **identified** (notice that the word uses **identity** as a root) by their height, color, voice, color of their eyes, age, and other characteristics, which were known by most of the community because it was small.

Your personal "identity" is a very interesting and complex construct.

Who are you?

You are first of all a unique entity made up of a one-of-a-kind DNA signature.

As a result you belong to a species.

You have specific physical characteristics, gender, size, skin color, shape, fingerprints, etc. These may define you as being from a certain lineage and probably ancestrally from a certain geographic location and society.

You are the product of birth (a combination of genetic material from a man and woman). Therefore, you may have attributes such as a name, family name, and other identifiers that make up part of who you are.

You have a birth date and birthplace. You are entitled to documentation that certifies all of this.

Depending on where you are born, you have residency and citizenship in a certain place and may be entitled to documents that entitle you to the privileges of that society and / or country. Among the documentation are identification papers such as a number used for transactions (Social Security Card), travel papers (passport), documents that entitle you to certain activities such as driving a vehicle (driver's license), or flying aircraft (pilot's license).

In addition, you also accrue a series of other traits that are added to your most basic identity such as an education, religion, distinguishing marks (birth marks, tattoos, marks caused by surgery or illness). You acquire dental characteristics that are added onto your natural dental structure – fillings, teeth pulled, caps, root canals. As you know, when all else about you is destroyed say in a fire, your dental record can still be used as your "ID card."

Your identity is further enhanced by education, degrees you earn, jobs you take, criminal and arrest records you accrue, medical records, marriage, widowhood or divorce, and military service.

In addition you may earn or be awarded financial privileges such as credit cards, a line of credit, or a home mortgage.

As you can see, "who is you" over time becomes a very complicated, rich, changing, and often convoluted reality. We all have a set of characteristics, some physical, some cultural or political (such as citizenship and voting rights), some transitory (credit or your criminal record, both of which can change constantly), some very, very permanent such as your DNA, your fingerprints, and your retina.

When we talk about identity theft, we are talking about a complex set of characteristics, some of which are very easy to impersonate or emulate (a school transcript) and some of which are more permanent. Even physical characteristics, which seem like the most profound and permanent are, obviously, also transitory such as hair, skin (smooth or wrinkled), and even things like how many extremities (legs and arms, fingers, ears) you have.

When a society sets about trying to monitor, track, and give certain rights to individuals based on their verifiable identity, it is, in fact, embarking on a very substantial challenge.

It's not easy to prove who you are and, on the other hand, in regard to many characteristics, it's pretty easy for someone to pretend to be you.

That's what this book is all about.

Let's look at the issue of identity a little differently.

Google "Human identity" on your computer. (http://www.google.com/)

What do you get?

We found a lot of very, very specific hits when Google's first major hit took us to Google Scholar. They had titles such as:

• Identity-by-descent and association mapping of a recessive gene for Hirschsprung disease on human chromosome 13q22

• The sequence of human caveolin reveals identity with VIP21, a component of transport vesicles.

• Quantitative determination of bone marrow transplant engraftment using fluorescent polymerase chain reaction primers for human identity markers

• Human identity testing with PCR-based systems by Hohoff C, Brinkmann B., Institut fur Rechtsmedizin, Universitat Munster, Germany "Large numbers of repetitive stretches of DNA are present within the human genome that are associated with human individuality due to their polymorphic character…"

What was interesting in these hits (beside the fact that we had no idea what these scientific articles were about!) was that they referred to DNA, the very specific markers of human traits.

Another hit took us to a basic but interesting site that talked about human identity not as the individual identity of a single person but as the identity of all humans taken together and looked at in comparison to other species.

"Like other complex organisms, people vary in size and shape, skin color, body proportions, body hair, facial features, muscle strength, handedness, and so on. But these differences are minor compared to the internal similarity of all humans, as demonstrated by the fact that people from anywhere in the world can physically mix on the basis of reproduction, blood transfusions, and organ transplants. Humans are indeed a single species. Furthermore, as great as cultural differences between groups of people seem to be, their complex languages, technologies, and arts distinguish them from any other species." http://www.project2061.org/publications/sfaa/online/chap6.htm

We found this interesting because it raises the question of how we distinguish between individual humans for purposes of identifying a single person and matching him/her to the appropriate and accurate credit card, social security number, passport, bank account, hospital record, college transcript and diploma, job, marriage and so on.

We need to remember that the actual differences between people and individuals "are minor."

Yet, when we walk into a bank, store or airport, or log

on to a web site to transact business, the difference between "me" and "you" is expected to be very clear, distinct and unambiguous! In other words, not all old ladies or all people who look like Arabs are the same. The system is supposed to identify, from among millions of people, those who are a risk and separate them from those who are not.

To return to what we were discussing above, impersonation is not the only form of duplicating an identity. Classic document forgeries have been around since the first representational documents were created. These were often elaborate seals that would be pressed into melted wax to authenticate the origin and validity of a document. Seals could, of course, be forged and history is full of examples of these rather crude dissemblings of the truth.

Of course, written information about people has been collected and recorded for eons. This "data" was stored in repositories and consisted, depending on the period in human history, of clay tablets, tree bark, papyrus, sheepskins, and later mass-produced paper. We know from the historical record that this information was valuable to rulers and governments as data to levy taxes, draft people into the armies, keep track of financial and land transactions, and keep tables on the number, religion, and other demographics of individuals. No doubt data stealing and forging has taken place as long as humans have inhabited this planet.

In these past periods of history, analog - physically spatial techniques - were the only way to accomplish the trick of stealing data and identities. This required the culprit to physically snatch the clay tablet or the document from the filing cabinet. It meant skirting guards, breaking in, and leaving undetected. Of course we know that it happened with regularity, but it was usually difficult. Occasionally armies would march through and loot large amounts of this information, using or destroying it for nefarious purposes such as destroying ownership records in order to steal land, cattle, children, gold, wives, ships, or other goods.

Who has not heard of The Great Impostor, that master of impersonation and fraud who was able to pass himself as a doctor, an airline pilot, a business magnate, and dozens of other personalities because he understood the human psyche and had such great talent for duplicating the persona of people in different professions. That's quite different than if he had actually stolen the background information and identification papers of, say, a real airline pilot and then passed himself off as that genuine aviator. That would have been identity theft. The other was "merely" impersonation!

We found the following discussion very informative and relevant to our interest in personal identities and identity theft. In their article "Dynamics of Human Identity", Vladimir Dimitrov and Kalevi Kopra, of the University of Western Sydney-Hawkesbury argue that a distinct and unique identity for every person is largely a bureaucratic, government initiative to better monitor, track, tax and control people.

Society prefers to operate with fixed identities - they help to divide people into groups, to 'push' the groups into separated "boxes" and computer files (hierarchical or nested into one another), to label these boxes and files with names, numbers and codes, and then to do with them all sorts of manipulations. And above all, to exercise control.

Social control cannot function without building a well

structured system of fixed identities. It is easier to exercise control over fixed group identities than over variable individual identities which are elusive, flexible, resistant to control, open for change, evolution and growth. When squeezed into a fixed group identity, individual identity is in danger to lose its uniqueness and to become a mediocre entity in a majority of 'they-say' people, easily susceptible for manipulation and corruption.

Living individual identities are chaotic - extremely sensitive to changes (however tiny they might appear) occurring in both external and internal human conditions, unpredictable and, therefore, free. Fixed identities are locked into pre-designed ordered patterns - insensitive to changes, easily predictable and, therefore, unfree.

All kinds of control tools like tax file numbers, license numbers, passports, identity cards, certificates, permission for residence, visas, etc. are extensively put into operation in to-day's society in order to keep human identities fixed.

Any fixed identity easily becomes a string of alphanumeric characters compressed to satisfy the requirements of a variety of computer data-bases. Once captured by the computer, human identities become imprisoned for life in a System from which no escape exists. This is The System of Fixed Identities - a great relief for all kinds of surveillance authorities in *human society.*

http://www.zulenet.com/VladimirDimitrov/pages/identity.html

In recent times, the thefts of information have also included the "harvesting" of discarded information as in "dumpster diving" or "garbage raiding" - looking for those pieces of paper containing accounts, social security numbers, and other treasures to be abused by criminals.

Theft of information has also taken place at the nexus between analog activity, getting money from an ATM machine, and the new technology of the future, stealing a person's PIN number and then withdrawing money from his/her account. In some cases, this involved the simple technique of having a long zoom lens on a camera and shooting video of the person logging into his/her account. In other cases, it moved over into the world of high tech, installing a "fake" swipe card reader on a real ATM machine, capturing (recording) the information from the card and from the person's keystrokes on the machine, and then using this information to access many people's accounts.

Then no more than a few decades ago along came information technology (IT), computers, and more recently the Internet.

As they say, that changed everything!

As we will see in the subsequent chapter, IT has become a geometrically greater opportunity for identity theft because of its awesome speed, the sheer volume of information that can be simultaneously high jacked, and the almost unbelievable fact that information can be accessed and stolen from thousands of miles away, anonymously! The security weaknesses and vulnerabilities of Microsoft Windows and the fact that it is the huge 800-pound gorilla of operating systems, has made computing very unsafe. By contrast, the much smaller Mac operating system has been far less a target for malice and crime.

The lesson of this chapter is that throughout human history the identity of people has been a unique marker that set "me" apart from "you." Like many species, we are an amazingly individualistic lot. It is each human being who has a name, a history, and who also has property and rights. Taking someone's identity and using it for ones own lucrative benefit has always been with us. Protecting our "us" from thieves has always been a premium value for humans. It remains so in the 21st century. Succeeding in protecting "me" against "them" however, has become as difficult, maybe much more difficult, than it has ever been since humans first took names and started accumulating stuff.

The battle continues as it always has throughout history, but the struggle grows bigger as opportunities for stealing people's money and names proliferate with technology.

Identity Theft in the News – Recent History

Let's bring this history closer.

Do a search on the Internet and you quickly realize the vast range and complexity of the issue of Internet fraud and identity theft. The following were the most interesting and timely stories we found. We share them because there is no teacher like reality and these stories illustrate the range and complexity of identity theft risks we all face.

Case study # 1. "REAL ID: Today's driver's licenses provide little protection against fraud, identity theft or terrorist attack."

"The object of tightening security provisions against terrorist attack is to get the most safety for the least money and inconvenience." The REAL ID rules announced … by the Department of Homeland Security come close to doing that.

The current practice of making airline passengers show

a driver's license does the opposite, producing maximum aggravation without much elevating the level of security. In a press release accompanying the new regulations, Homeland Security Secretary Michael Chertoff pointed out that the 9/11 hijackers had acquired 30 drivers' licenses and IDs and used 364 aliases.

By Dec. 1, 2014, all Americans under 50 would have to acquire a new driver's license that would be more difficult to forge. Americans older than 50 would have an additional three years — tacit recognition that few people over 50 have the energy or inclination to mount a terrorist attack against their countrymen.

Before issuing one of the new, more secure licenses, state authorities would have to make sure that the applicant was who he said he was and was not an undocumented immigrant or criminal bent on fraud.

The American Civil Liberties Union objects to the new regulations on grounds that they would create a giant national database vulnerable to identity theft. Chertoff told Chronicle editors Friday that the system would use only existing databases that would be fortified and be less vulnerable than they are now.

Houston Chronicle.com, Interview with Chertoff,
http://www.chron.com/disp/story.mpl/editorial/5454204.html

Case study # 2. "Cops: Carle Place worker nabbed in ID theft", BY JOSEPH MALLIA

A clerk at a Carle Place furniture store stole customers' credit card information and racked up more than $10,000 in fraudulent purchases, Nassau police said.

Megan Cambridge, 23, of 3305 Foster Ave Apt. 4F, Brooklyn, stole the credit information from customers at the Raymour & Flanigan furniture store at 275 Glen Cove Rd., police said in a report made public Monday.

Cambridge was arrested Saturday afternoon in Carle Place, according to the police report. She was charged with four counts each of grand larceny and identity theft and was arraigned in First District Court in Hempstead. Newsday, Jan 15, 2008

Case study # 3. "Colombian pleads guilty to internet-based ID theft scam" by Jim Carr

"A Colombian citizen pleaded guilty to a 16-count indictment involving an internet-based fraud scam intending to steal the personal information of more than 600 people."

Carr reports that "Mario Simbaqueba Bonilla, 40, admitted in U.S. District Court in Miami to illegally installing keystroke logging software on computers in hotel business centers and Internet lounges around the world. The software collected the personal information, including passwords and other personal identifying information that the victims used to access their bank, payroll, brokerage and other accounts online."

"Bonilla used the data he intercepted from his victims -- mostly guests at U.S. hotels -- to steal or divert money from victims' bank, payroll and mortgage accounts into other accounts he created in the names of other victims. Then, via what the U.S. Justice Department (DOJ) called "a complex series of electronic transactions designed to cover his trail," Simbaqueba Bonilla transferred the stolen money to credit, cash or debit-card accounts and had the cards mailed to himself and others at commercial mailing addresses."

Most of Bonilla's identity theft activity, which was carried out from Colombia, was aimed at U.S. residents and included Defense Department personnel. He used the ill gotten gains to buy " ... expensive electronics and luxury travel accommodations in various countries including Hong Kong, Turks and Caicos, France, Jamaica, Italy, Chile and the United States."

"Unfortunately, this is not an isolated case," R. Alexander Acosta, U.S. Attorney for the Southern District of Florida, said in a prepared statement. "The Internet is an outstanding tool, but it is vulnerable. Criminals like Bonilla use the Internet to steal our banking and personal data, and then our money. When you travel, think twice before entering personal or financial data on a public computer."

He was arrested in the US and had come on an airline ticket bought with stolen funds. The DOJ also reports that he had a laptop purchased with stolen funds. On that computer were the names, passwords and other personal and financial information of more than 600 people.

"It would be interesting to know if Bonilla used the unsecured, wireless, electronic transmissions of the hotel guests (unsecured wireless is often available in hotel lobbies) to also access or capture information," R.M. Tracy, a former FBI special agent and the founder of the Privacy Trust Group, a security consultancy, told SCMagazineUS.com. "If the hotel computers were infected with keylogging programs or otherwise not effectively secured, this could have added to the problem. Why was it mainly hotel guests who were victims? This begs more questions than it answers about what Bonilla was really doing and how he was doing it."

"Consumers should be wary of accessing bank accounts from shared public computers that could have keystroke loggers or other malware on them," Ed Mierzwinski, consumer program director of the U.S. Public Interest Research Group (USPRIG), a consumer advocacy organization, told SCMagazineUS.com. "Consumers should also be wary of accessing their accounts while using their own computers on unsecured Wi-Fi or other public networks."

SC magazine on Line, http://www.scmagazineus.com/
Colombian-pleads-guilty-to-internet-based-ID-theft-scam/
article/104161/

Case study # 4. "Senior Citizens Vulnerable To ID Theft Scams: New E-Mail Circulating Poses As IRS"

MIAMI -- Anyone with a telephone or a computer is a target of identity theft, but senior citizens are even more vulnerable.

"Seniors come from a different world -- a different era -- so they're very trusting," said Carmen Caldwell of Citizens Crime Watch.

It wasn't hard for Local 10's Sasha Andrade to find a victim of identity theft in a group of elderly people.

"They called me and asked me what magazines do I like," said Denise Gray.

Instead of receiving Rachel Ray's magazine and other cooking magazines, "Next thing I knew they was drawing money out of my account," said Gray.

Criminals have posed as vendors, as a sweepstakes and now they're pretending to be the Internal Revenue Service.

"There's an e-mail going out and you think its IRS," said Caldwell.

The e-mail claims the government owes the victim money.

"It tells you where to click, and it tells you, you know, to put in (personal) information," said Caldwell.

Citizens Crime Watch warns everyone, especially seniors, to be careful and not to give out personal information unless they know whom they're giving it to.

Source: Local10.com

When we Googled the phrase "Identity Theft" in 2005 we got **9,740,000** hits. In 2008 that number had risen to

16,800,000. Google is a great search engine and both the sheer number of hits and the impressive increase over a two-year period revealed to us that this problem is very significant as a general concern.

Clearly then, ID theft has come into its own and it behooves us to pay attention to it and develop some new behavior to secure our own vital statistics and numbers. It also is important that we as a nation respond appropriately to the problem of ID theft, a topic we will cover in a subsequent chapter.

Moreover, institutions and organizations in the United States – corporations, colleges and universities, hospitals, doctors, small businesses, airlines, banks and financial institutions, sports clubs, and non-profit groups must also raise the level of protection for the vital, valuable, and personal information that has accumulated like so much archeological material throughout our society.

Case Study # 5 – The Largest ID Theft Case in the United States

The following is an interesting case study that we want to share with you. It details one way that identity theft occurs. It also informs you of the legal aspects of ID theft prosecution, which we feel is a very important and largely understudied part of this crisis. When this case came down in 2002, it was a shockingly large ID theft case. If only we had known at the time that this was just the tip of an iceberg which would grow enormously over the coming years.

What is also disheartening about the case is that it was an inside job. It proves beyond a doubt that no matter how careful consumers are with their sensitive data they can do nothing about most id theft attacks against them. It also underscores again the importance of having aggressive law enforcement and recourse to legal counsel to press charges and both resolve the liabilities incurred when id information is abused and misused and also to punish id theft criminals.

U.S. Announces What Is Believed The Largest Identity Theft Case In American History; Losses Are In The Millions

JAMES B. COMEY, the United States Attorney for the Southern District of New York, and KEVIN P. DONOVAN, the Assistant Director in Charge of the New York Field Office of the FBI, today announced the arrest of a defendant, PHILIP CUMMINGS, in what authorities believe to be the largest identity theft case in U.S. history. Mr. COMEY also announced the arrest of LINUS BAPTISTE and the guilty plea of HAKEEM MOHAMMED in related cases.

In a Complaint unsealed today, the United States charged PHILIP CUMMINGS with wire fraud and conspiracy in connection with his participation in a massive identity theft scheme that spanned nearly three years and involved more than 30,000 victims. As alleged in the Complaint, CUMMINGS worked at Teledata Communications Inc. ("TCI"), a company in Long Island that provided the computerized means for banks and other entities to obtain consumer credit information from the three commercial credit history bureaus Equifax, Experian and TransUnion. TCI provided software and other computerized devices to its client companies that enabled these companies, through the use of confidential computer passwords and subscriber codes, to access and download credit reports of consumers for legitimate business purposes.

As alleged in the Complaint, CUMMINGS worked at TCI

from about mid-1999 through about March 2000 as a Help-Desk *employee, and was responsible for helping TCI's clients. As such, he had access to these companies' confidential passwords and codes. With these codes, he had the ability to access and download credit reports himself, it was charged.*
http://www.usdoj.gov/criminal/cybercrime/cummingsIndict.htm

Cummings was sentenced to 14 years in jail for ID theft. In his column on the Internet, Digger writes:

"If you think this is bad, wait until they find all the ID theft happening in India. With all the outsourced data they have access to -- including medical records, credit card data, bank account information, tax returns and US government data -- it wouldn't be hard. On top of that, consider the average pay for a worker over there and the un-accountability and you have a recipe for disaster. It's bound to happen sooner or later and it will be on a much larger scale."

He may have a point there! Be prepared.

Case Study

ID Theft Potential from Old Records

In a blog entry January 16, 2008 titled "ID Theft Gets Real" Tom Shoop writes that

"Most of the recent scary stories about the loss or theft of federal employees' personally identifiable information involve the theoretical possibility that such data could be used for fraudulent purposes. Now comes a story where it came much closer to really happening."

The story is that on Jan. 5, 2008 four people were arrested in Bensalem Township, Pa., for attempted identity fraud. One of the suspects had two pages of a 1994 report that included the names, Social Security numbers, birth dates, salary information and other data about roughly 100 employees with last names starting with the letter B of the Naval Surface Warfare Center Dahlgren Division in Dahlgren, VA.

According to the Richmond Times-Dispatch, officials don't know whether the suspects have all of the pages of the 13 1/2-year-old report, but they indicated that as many as 10,000 employees may be at risk of identity theft.

At the time of the 1994 report, Dahlgren provided the human resources office for five Navy agencies at Dahlgren, as well others. Dahlgren officials say they notified employees on Jan. 10 of the situation by e-mail. Those who may have been affected accordingly could have worked at the Naval Facilities Command, NSWC Dahlgren, NSWC White Oak, Md., NSWC Panama City, Fla., the Joint Warfare Analysis Center, the Naval Space Command and the Aegis Training and Readiness Center.

The Secret Service is investigating this case now. Normally, according to the officials, Dahlgren disposes of unneeded personal information documents by shredding them.

The Navy has set up a call center at 1-800-352-7967 to provide more information.

http://blogs.govexec.com/fedblog/2008/01/id_theft_gets_real.php
http://www.inrich.com/cva/ric/news.apx.-content-articles-RTD-
2008-01-15-0194.html

This story is a perfect example of what we have been lecturing about in our ID theft protection seminars – the disposal of old records.

Since Social Security numbers started to be used for identification, hundreds of millions of records in files have been collected and stored all over the United States. These "old" and often "forgotten" records are in fact nothing but identity risk time bombs. They remain dormant for many, many years, but the explosive quality of the information on all these forms stays "fresh" because it is timeless. In some cases it could even be used after the people on the records are dead so long as the age of the victim does not exceed the human life span.

More disturbingly, we are now discovering that US and Canadians sensitive information is scattered all over the world at embassies, military facilities, airports, and private companies. We even recently discovered a whole file cabinet of American passport numbers that were photocopied by the front desk of a hotel in Rome, Italy (as required by Italian law according to the concierge) and shoved into a cabinet. These passport pages have all the information necessary to do the legitimate owners a lot of damage.

Now multiply the filing cabinet of that one hotel by the hundreds or thousands all over the world where you almost always have to show your passport upon checking in. In the case of most European countries including Italy, you actually must leave the passport with the front desk clerk and pick it up later, often the next day.

These old records, as was the case with the Naval Surface Warfare Center old documents, should be shredded. However, there are also many laws that require information to be kept for purposes of audits, historical record keeping, verifying employment histories, and for other management reasons.

In fact, we recently talked to a former Internal Revenue Service manager who pointed out that the IRS has requirements on the length of time you must keep tax records that vary from three years to INDEFINITLY! You can find out how long by going to the IRS web site http://www.irs.gov/ and searching for this information. These tax records contain Social Security numbers and all kinds of information on the person, on employees, on consultants, children and dependents.

People don't have room to keep all these records and it is now very common practice (again according to our IRS colleague) for people to put all that information into old liquor bottle or grocery store produce boxes and then stick them in their storage locker. We all know how secure those rental lockers are! The Dallas Morning News had a lengthy report of the police work that broke a ring of thieves who stole from storage facilities. The Sherburne County Minnesota Sheriff's Department responded to numerous theft reports from storage lockers in Big Lake and Baldwin Townships. The Privacy Rights Clearinghouse lists storage lockers as a high risk for identity information theft.

Old documents and files, even analog paper files, represent an unseen and un-remembered threat to personal security. Moreover, they are often not in the consumer's possession but instead are under the stewardship of small time, low paid, unremarkable clerks and employees. There is no solution to this problem (especially to the international mishandling of critical information documents). There is no "document shredding" agency or program. There are no penalties for leaving old filing cabinets sitting around with files in the drawers. Every day at junk and antique stores around the world, old filing cabinets and desks and armoires and other items are bought by someone, opened and inside them people find all kinds of cool stuff. Some of what they find are old records with personal information.

By the way privacyrights.org has a list of, sit down before we tell you, ..., 46 steps you must take to secure your personal identity! We have examined this list and concluded that if a person were to actually practice these 46 steps, the average consumer should quit work, give up any family life and become a full time guardian and defender of his or her personal information! http://www.privacyrights.org/fs/fs17-it.htm

The list includes these:

• "When you fill out loan or credit applications, find out how the company disposes of them." (Yeah, the 19-year-old, part time, Christmas season salesperson at Banana Republic where one of us applied for a credit card recently – they require a Social Security number on the form – knows the identity protection and security policy of the company!)

• "Demand that financial institutions adequately safeguard your data." ("Mr. Johnson, I expect you as the bank manager to give me a tour of the security algorithm and safe lock-down facilities where my account information will be managed. Also, give me a briefing of the sensitive data security training program the bank has for all of its employees and a report on previous data losses!")

• "Use a gel pen for writing checks. Experts say that gel ink contains tiny particles of color that are trapped in the paper, making check washing more difficult."

• "Each month, carefully review your credit card, bank and phone statements, including cellular phone bills". (Ok, so let us get this right. YOU want us to "balance" our checkbooks? And look over all the expenses and compare charges against the credit card receipts from Two Thumbs Up Bar and Grill, Starbucks, the Quick Trip Gas Station, the Mars Bar I charged at the college snack shop ….?! What about all the stores where you charge and they don't have you sign anything anymore OR give you a receipt for the charge?!)

•   "To minimize the amount of information a thief can steal, do not carry extra credit cards, debit cards, your Social Security card, birth certificate or passport in your wallet or purse." (What do you mean by "extra"? Like, I have a Visa, a Master Card, an Amex Card, my bank debit card, my Credit Union debit card, my Sam's Club Corporate card, well you get the idea. Which of these is the "extra" credit card!?)

When we asked some of our colleagues about these and some of the other 46 steps they laughed and said they could never do this. ("What is a "gel pen"? I can never find ANY pen in my purse anyway and use the one at the bank," one of our associates said).

So what's the answer to this?

We should as a society make every effort to encourage the secure shredding of all unnecessary and dated files. We should insist that these shredded files be disposed of in a secure manner.

Chapter 3 reviews in detail the major types of identity theft and has some very interesting material on medical Id theft, which is a major problem in the United States.

CHAPTER 3

FINANCIAL, MEDICAL, CHARACTER, AND "SYNTHETIC" IDENTITY THEFT

"Atlanta, GA -11/16/07, MATTHEW BEVAN COX, 38, formerly of Nashville, Atlanta, and Tampa, was sentenced today by United States District Judge Timothy C. Batten, Sr., on charges of mortgage fraud, identity theft, passport fraud and violation of the terms of his probation. "Cox will now be serving the long prison sentence he deserves for his crimes," said United States Attorney David E. Nahmias in Atlanta. "While the subject of a nationwide manhunt, Cox repeatedly used the stolen identities of minor children, the homeless and others to place multiple fraudulent loans on the same property without the knowledge or consent of the true owners. His crimes resulted in clouded property titles in several states with years of unresolved litigation, a trail of over 100 victims, and millions of dollars in losses that cannot be recovered."

For **"The Rest of the Case"** go to the end of the chapter.

As the summary of the Cox case above suggests, the outright theft of identity information can occur in odd ways and spares no one, even children and the homeless.

In this chapter we will briefly review four types of problems that can make you a victim of identity loss. Financial or credit card, medical, loss of your character, and synthetic identity theft are serious business and are the most likely areas in which you may suffer the consequences of loss or theft of critical information. The latest information we were able to obtain from the Department of Justice in 2007 shows the following:

The Federal Trade Commission's Consumer Sentinel collects information about consumer fraud and identity theft from the FTC and over 150 other organizations, including the Federal Bureau of Investigation, U.S. Secret Service, fourteen Attorney Generals Offices, and various State and local law enforcement agencies. According to the FTC report, Consumer Fraud and Identity Theft Complaint Data (January-December 2006) (2007). Findings from an analysis of those complaints include -

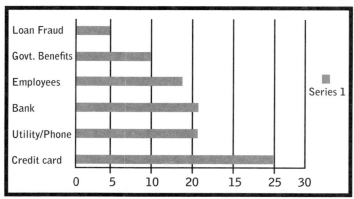

• Of the complaints received during calendar year 2006, 64% represented fraud and 36% were identity theft complaints.

• Credit card fraud (25%) was the most common form of reported identity theft followed by phone or utilities fraud (16%), bank fraud (16%), and employment fraud (14%). See Chart on page 38.

• "Electronic Fund Transfer" related identity theft was the most frequently reported type of identity theft bank fraud during calendar year 2006.

The metropolitan areas with the highest per capita rates of reported identity theft are Napa, California; Madera, California; and McAllen-Edinburg-Mission, Texas.

http://www.ncjrs.gov/spotlight/identity_theft/facts.html

Let's examine these major areas of risk in more detail.

1. Financial identity theft

Credit card fraud is the most common form at 28 percent of all cases followed by bank fraud at 18 percent. The criminal will set up accounts in your name using alternative addresses, use your existing bank account at another branch (with the driver's license they obtained in your name with their picture), borrow money on your home, buy a car or furniture in another town, drain your online stockbrokerage accounts; the list is endless. From the article "Who Is "You"? Identity Theft," by Michael McCoy.

The vandals in their nasty furs, flashing their massive swords and flailing spiky swing-balls (that's what I call them), burst into the department store ready to loot and pillage. Just as they are about to steal hapless customers' funds, they realize that one of the shoppers has a Capital One credit card. The music stops. The barbarians drop their arms and slump, realizing that their mission has been thwarted by an impenetrable security system that makes your credit, your cash, and your identity safe and secure. In the latest episode the Huns are actually now unemployed because they can no longer loot and they have taken jobs in shoe stores, and their leader, now tame and depressed, runs a kiddy train at an amusement park.

Don't get me wrong. I love these ads. They are clever and the vandals are suitably nasty yet sorry characters since their mission is foiled every time because of the excellent security of your friendly plastic money purveyor.

What's bizarre and in some ways infuriating is the fact that the ads continue to run at the same moment that identity theft is reaching alarming proportions. Hackers have penetrated unprecedented numbers of financial institutions; credit card numbers on computer tapes have mysteriously vanished from delivery trucks in the US and abroad.

What's up here?

Truth be told, the banking and financial services industry is not only in denial but is also a great example of form over function. We are all used to a lack of truth in advertising. Who can forget the days when cereal companies put toys in their cereal boxes? On TV they used clever angles, sophisticated lenses, and close ups that made the toys look HUGE. Several studies showed that when kids actually ripped open the box, and fished out the toy, they were usually very disappointed because the actual prize was tiny and shoddy. The lesson of all advertising, the mantra of Madison Avenue, has been to overpromise and use slick advertising and packaging to sell.

Have you ever bought a piece of software in a box (the size of a cereal box) only to find that it's 90% box and a slim CD inside? In fact, have you ever pulled out the package of cereal inside the actual cereal box and found that there are four inches more box than cereal inside? (The box says something like "product may settle in shipping" in tiny print).

The principle guiding most financial services is "overpromise in a subtle and legal way." This is more or less how we picture the problem:

YOU have been selected for our new Advanced Complex Titanium credit card at only 2% interest rate for the first year!

The "fine print" reads:

Subsequent rates may be set at the rate of inflation in Zimbabwe or interest rates for the new currency in Iraq, whichever is higher. We are not responsible if this unsolicited card offer is stolen out of your mailbox and used by someone else to buy stuff in your name and then destroy your credit rating for at least 5 years and cost you over $20,000 to fix.

The tragedy is that in the area of finances, stolen credit cards or credit card numbers are only one potential disaster facing you – the tip of the iceberg.

However they do it, crooks can highjack your identity to borrow money, apply for credit cards, and spend, spend, spend, in your name. In the "system" you are indistinguishable from whoever has grabbed your good name, your credit rating, your financial profile. As far as the banks and credit companies know, YOU are suddenly spending like crazy and not paying any of your bills. You are now a credit risk and you will not get any more credit from the bank, credit card companies, mortgage companies, car dealers, the grocery store, in fact, from anyone.

Another series of funny and clever TV commercials for yet another bank and its credit cards shows people speaking about their recent purchases in voices that don't match the character on the TV – a huge nasty-looking tattooed guy speaks with a woman's voice; a nice-looking woman talks like a cool young guy. You get the idea. The person speaking has stolen someone's credit card and is now living it up at the expense of the legitimate owner. The only problem is that this **particular bank** has a shameful record in protecting its customers credit, yet continues to tout its concern for and success in protecting your financial security!

As a side bar, how come the news media doesn't focus more fiercely on identity theft? Hmmm, maybe the tens of millions in advertising revenue subtly influence what they report?

And, how come Congress has not aggressively legislated regulations that force the financial services industry to:

1. Invest in high-level security,

2. Report to a government agency and the public every security breach and identity theft, and .

3. Make companies responsible and criminally liable for using, selling, and sharing inaccurate personal information about individuals whether the information was purchased from an aggregator or collected on their own. The law could make the last company or the first company to have used this false information the responsible party.

Perhaps it has to do with the fact that banks and financial services companies are huge donors to campaigns and have some of the most powerful Washington lobbyists swarming all over Congress to protect their interests.

2. Medical identity theft

"Joe Ryan got a collection notice from a billing agency for Littleton Adventist Hospital near Denver, Colorado. The hospital wanted payment for surgery totaling $41,188. Ryan, a Vail pilot, had never set foot in that hospital. Obviously there was some mistake. "I thought it was a joke," says Ryan. But when he called the billing agency, nobody laughed. Someone named Joe Ryan, using Ryan's Social Security number, had indeed been admitted for surgery. A busy man, Ryan was trying to get his new sightseeing business, Rocky Mountain Biplane Adventures, off the ground. He figured clearing this up would take just a few phone calls.

Two years later, Ryan continues to suffer from the damage to his credit rating and still doesn't know if his medical record has been cleared of erroneous information. "I'm desperately trying not to go bankrupt," he says.

Joe Ryan was the victim of a little-known but frightening type of consumer fraud that is on the rise: medical identity theft".

2008 search, http://www.safetysend.com/Medical-Identity-Theft.htm

Senator Hillary Clinton, Democrat from New York, and Senator Bill Frist, Republican from Tennessee appeared on TV announcing their joint proposal to computerize the medical records of all Americans. The goal is to make the management of health care more efficient and cost effective and more "portable" – i.e. if you live in El Paso but get sick in

Boston, the local emergency room or physician can call up your medical records electronically and treat you appropriately.

This is great and, like everything else in the United States, computerized information and integrated, networked databases must eventually come to the medical profession. If your experience is like ours, your doctor has a messy folder filled with paper, scribbled notes, x-rays, blood tests, and who knows what else.

What struck us was that not once did the interviewer ask Senator Frist or Clinton about security, about the risk of medical records being hacked and made public or stolen for other nefarious purposes. You have a vivid imagination. Just imagine all the risks of having your medical history, your prescriptions, your treatments and surgeries, your psychiatric treatments and mental condition, slip into the hands of people who are unauthorized to see them.

Most of us overlook this potential criminal aspect of digital records. It occurs in numerous ways: employees of hospitals copying your files for personal information; others using your social security number to have procedures done like surgery or even an AIDS/HIV test; people checking into the emergency room under your name so they can kindly pass on the cost directly to you. Another reason for stealing records may be to obtain an elderly person's insurance, Medicare/Medicaid or prescription drug benefits. Imagine if you went to your pharmacist and he told you your prescription had already been filled in a neighboring community, another state, or even in another country (our pharmacist fills prescriptions for traveling clients from our community all the time) and he could not fill it again.

Here are some of the risks of unsecured medical and health risks:

• Employers could screen out job applicants with health problems that might pose risks or costs.

• Insurance companies would be able to reject applicants with health histories or conditions that would raise their costs.

• Public figures and candidates for office could have embarrassing problems depending on what information was in their records, for example STD's, psychiatric problems, etc.

Medical Consequences of Credit Rating – Risk Scoring in America

"When Jane Doe suddenly collapsed in the lobby of her five star hotel in Beijing, the concierge immediately dialed the ambulance as he had been trained. Gold Star Emergency Services arrived and whisked her to the best hospital in the city, which was the hotel chain's policy. As Jane was checked into the ER, the attending staffer entered her name and passport number into a wireless tablet and clicked on the "crdt chck" icon. Within seconds the "credit score" bar for Jane appeared and it was at the red end of the scale. Bad news. Red=bad credit rating. Bright green on the opposite end= great credit rating. Jane was given a quick and perfunctory check up as required by the US-China bilateral medical agreement and then discharged, put into a taxicab, sent back to the hotel and advised to get a full check up when she returned to the US."

Fictional narrative of what could happen.
Medical debt is a big problem in the United States.
The 2005 American Hospital Association, "Heath Fo-

rum," Annual Survey of US hospitals reported that 4936 hospitals reported a total "Uncompensated Care" of $28.8 billion dollars, which accounted for 5.6% of total expenses in these hospitals. Some of this was bad debt and the remainder was charity care.

Of adults under the age of 65:

- 1 in 3 had problems related to medical bills or accrued medical debt (34%).
- 1 in 5 had medical bills or accrued medical debt they were paying off over time (21%).
- The vast majority (62%) of these individuals were insured when the bill was incurred.
  Commonwealth Fund Biennial Health Insurance Survey

The "Kaiser Commission on Medicaid and Uninsured 2003 Health Insurance Survey" reported that an estimated 58 million adults are at risk of incurring medical bills they may not be able to afford. 1 in 6 adults with private insurance - 17.6 million adults report having substantial problems paying their medical bills.

How do businesses and the medical profession determine who are good customers and who are bad risks?

Human beings have evaluated risk since the dawn of civilization. Using intuition and past experience, people have always decided how risky it was to cross a river with thin ice, approach a large toothy cat too closely, travel through the territory of a neighboring tribe, or do business with someone you either knew or who was a stranger. Formal and statistical systems of designing "risk scores" were invented in the 1960's and have become very sophisticated especially since the advent of digital data mining, storing, analysis and sharing. Your financial behavior and record is no longer of concern only to the local clothing store, bank or grocery. You can now be risk scored from anywhere in the world. One form of risk scoring is your medical risk score. This can be a measure of prior conditions, your age, weight, genetic, and other risk factors. It can also be your medical financial credit record.

In a frightening article on his blog Red Tape Chronicles, Friday, January 18, 2008, MSNB's Bob Sullivan reported on a new project called 'MedFICO". His blog is titled "The doctor will see your credit now" and it is of direct and great significance to our concerns about the consequences of identity theft. Here are some excerpts from Sullivan's blog. Because there are so many responses to this blog, we recommend that everyone go to the web site and read the original post and the angry responses.

http://redtape.msnbc.com/2008/01/the-doctor-wi-1.html#posts

"MedFICO" as described by Sullivan and others could be a frightening connection between people's credit score and their medical treatment. Sullivan writes:

"The folks who invented the credit score for lenders are hard at work developing a similar tool for hospitals and other health care providers. The project, dubbed "MedFICO" in some early press reports, will aid hospitals in assessing a patient's ability to pay their medical bills. But privacy advocates are worried that the notorious errors that have caused frequent criticism of the credit system will also cause trouble with any attempt to create a health-related risk score. They also fear that a low score might impact the quality of the

health care that patients receive."

A spokesman for Healthcare Analytics, Tim Hurley said criticism of the planned health credit score is wrong, product is still in development, and the term MedFICO is inaccurate and this product really does not exist.

But there is something afoot, so if MedFICO or a similar product were to become a reality how would all of this work. Since private business information and practices are often confidential and proprietary, we can only speculate, but Sullivan writes that

"Several published reports have described Healthcare Analytics product as a MedFICO score, computed in a way that would be familiar to those who've used credit scores. The firm is gathering payment history information from large hospitals around the country, according to a magazine called Inside ARM, aimed at "accounts receivable management" professionals. It will then analyze that data to predict how likely patients will be to pay future medical bills. As with credit reports and scores, patients who've failed to pay past bills will be deemed less likely to pay future bills."

Clearly this suggests a potential problem for patients with bad credit ratings. This is a very serious moral issue in a country such as the United States where medical care is provided to those who have health insurance, who have strong credit ratings and lines of credit and can afford to pay for healthcare on their own, or who are covered by some other health plan. Besides the ethical question of who should receive health care, it also raises the specter of patients who have had their credit and identity stolen and misused (and who don't know that this has happened) being denied the type of medical care they deserve.

Of course the Health Insurance Portability and Accountability Act (HIPAA), enacted by the U.S. Congress in 1996, establishes special rights for consumers. It regulates the availability and breadth of group and individual health insurance plans and prohibits any group health plan from creating eligibility rules or assessing premiums for individuals in the plan based on health status, medical history, genetic information, or disability. This rule does not apply to private individual insurance. HIPAA also has complex privacy provisions, which would apply to health credit ratings.

In the United States, the poor and those with no medical coverage are dumped on pubic hospitals many of which are going bankrupt. This problem needs to be resolved in the political and policy arena at the local, state, and federal government levels.

For the rich in the USA, health care has never been and will not be a problem in the future. They simply pay for it. And, the wealthy don't worry about having their credit rating destroyed by identity theft because they have id theft insurance and they have an army of lawyers standing by to fix the problem, prosecute and convict the criminals who have attacked their identity, and people who will quickly restore everything to normal.

So the issue of a new credit score specifically for medical creditworthiness will affect the middle class and especially those who do not have good oversight of their credit and their personal ID information. This means a vast majority of Americans should start worrying about the new techniques that are coming (even if MedFICO is not the product to do so) and that will allow health care providers to scrutinize patient's financial scores.

Pam Dixon, of the World Privacy Forum was quoted by Sullivan as saying, "This is a bad idea and I don't think this benefits the consumer at all. And what about victims of medical ID theft? Are we going to deny treatment to these people because they have a terrible MedFICO score?"

One of the huge problems with all of this is that a great number of American consumers' credit scores are wrong. The Consumer Federation did a study some years ago and found the following:

"Millions of Americans could pay more for - or be denied - credit, insurance, or utilities because of inaccurate credit scores, according to a new study, Credit Score Accuracy and Implications for Consumers, released this morning by the Consumer Federation of America (CFA) and the National Credit Reporting Association (NCRA).

Research for the study, conducted during the summer of 2002, analyzed the credit scores of more than 500,000 consumers, and extensively reviewed the files of more than 1,700 individuals, maintained by the three major credit repositories - Equifax, Experian, and Trans Union. Nearly 200 million Americans have credit files.

The analysis of the scores in 502,623 merged credit files reveals that 29 percent of these consumers had scores with a range of at least 50 points, while four percent of the consumers had score ranges of at least 100 points. The average range of the three scores was 41 points, and the median range was 35 points. Credit scores range from approximately 400 to 800.

"This frequent huge discrepancy in scores reveals the

importance of consumers being able to quickly learn and correct inaccuracies," said J. Robert Hunter, CFA's Director of Insurance. "Creditors should be required to provide to consumers, charged anything other than the best available rate or denied credit, a copy of credit reports free of charge, then to reconsider their decision based on any corrections," he added.

http://forum.creditcourt.com/discus/messages/10/624. html

As we indicated above consumers need to monitor their credit, find discrepancies and inaccuracies, and quickly correct mistakes before they proliferate into a person's personal record.

The insurance and health care industry on the other hand argues that bad credit is a huge problem in the health care field. Tenet Health ("Tenet Healthcare Corporation, through its subsidiaries, owns and operates acute care hospitals and related health care services.") is one of the backers of the MedFICO plan, which will collect payment data from hospital systems with a combined $100 billion in annual income. "Tenet told the Dallas Morning News it had $433 million in bad debts as of the third quarter of this year, one-fourth of it in the form of insurance deductibles patients wouldn't or couldn't pay." Of course, bad debts at hospitals and doctors are more than just the problem of care facilities that get stuck with unpaid bills. It produces a huge inflationary pressure on medical care as providers pass on the bad bills to their "good" customers.

Column, December 12th, 2007, **"Worried about your medFICO score"** by Dana **Blankenhorn**, http://health-care.zdnet.com/?p=570

The problem of bad debt in health care is serious business. Therefore, although it is a bit dated in terms of the statistics, we want to share with you the testimony "Medical Bad Debt – A Growing Public Health Crisis" by Nancy Kane, Professor, Harvard Business School, Boston, Massachusetts at the House Ways and Means Committee, US Congress. She started her testimony by pointing out that "Medical debt is the second-leading cause of personal bankruptcy." Sullivan also reported that, "Linda Foley, who runs the Identity Theft Resource Center, also pointed to the problem of Medical ID theft, which now hits 250,000 people each year, according to the Federal Trade Commission. Identity theft victims frequently find it difficult to clean their credit reports of errors; she feared medical ID theft victims might face the same fate."

http://waysandmeans.house.gov/hearings.
asp?formmode=view&id=1686

We hope that this brief discussion has been informative and confirms our argument in this entire book: you need to have an accurate and protected credit and personal identity history. Now, more than ever before it is important to be a smart identity consumer. If a system of medical credit checking ever becomes reality, your health and your very life could depend on an accurate repository of identity data on you.

Medical identity protection has become a very important concern for civil liberties, privacy, and identity protection. Most of us come into contact with medical facilities only rarely. We therefore felt it would be informative to have someone who works specifically in the health field to share some insights with us. We were very pleased that Brad Smith agreed to write the following insights for this book.

Hospitals Make My Identity Nervous!
Brad Smith, RN,MCNPS,CISSP,NSA-IAM

I'm a Registered Nurse so you think I'd be Ok with the way hospitals do things. It's not the patients' care that worries me - it's the security of the medical facility and the records that contain my identity. Why worry? Because I know that the vast number of patient records lost each year contains enough data for someone else to start a new life. At your expense!

Lots of people seem to have this same worry, so we have passed laws to try and better protect medical records, threatened jail time for executives and made preventing medical identity theft a high priority. Yet most facilities have failed in their security mission. The law has become toothless because of lax enforcement. And you and I are left with the damage of identity theft and little recourse.

Medical facilities have become the new target for thieves, hackers and general criminals. Why? Because that's where all YOUR data is. Data from multiple bank and credit card accounts plus tons of personal stuff is in your medical record. If you steal from one bank, you only get that bank's information. When people steal identity information from a medical site, they get your identity and most of your financial accounts. Hey, they even steal time to do nefarious things with your information because you're sick in bed and probably not checking your accounts anyway.

Don't think this problem is limited to just the medical

field. It's starting to crop up in every type of business. The worst part is that we are doing a really bad job of catching the people who commit these crimes. Here are the stats on cyber crime for 2006.

Total Number 2006 Reported Data Breach Incidents	327
Approximate Minimum Total # of PII Potentially Compromised in 2006	100,453,730
# Data-Breach Identity Thieves Sentenced in 2006	5
# Individual Victims of Sentenced Identity Thieves	238

Analysis prepared by Beth Rosenberg of Sandstorm.net

When you think about these numbers, that only 5 thieves were sentenced and 327 incidents occurred, you know the majority of people who committed these crimes are still out there.

How do you know whether hospitals have been victims of medical identify theft?

Most companies are required to notify the public if they have a security breech. Whether it's hackers, a wrong list posted on the web site, lost equipment, or something just plain stupid – hospitals are losing your identity at a growing rate.

Several web sites maintain a repository of publicly reported breaches. Please visit www.PrivacyRights.org, which maintains an active list of all publicly disclosed security breaches and how many records have been compromised. This site is depressing, when you realize the number of places with protected information about you and me that have had security breaches.

Let's survey the medical facilities that were breached from September to December of 2007. Now these are not small back-country places and they should have had the resources to be better prepared. If your medical facility is on this list, don't blame me! How's this for a list of Who's Who in the medical world? And this is only for the fourth quarter of 2007!

See table on following page.

Medical Data Breaches for Quarter 4, 2007

Date Facility	# of Records	
Dec. 18, 2007	Pennsylvania Department of Aging (Harrisburg, PA)	21,000
Dec. 17, 2007	West Penn Allegheny Health System (Pittsburgh, PA)	42,000
Dec. 10, 2007	Sutter Lakeside Hospital (Lakeport, CA)	45,000
Dec. 07, 2007	Beacon Medical Services (Aurora, CO)	0
Dec. 07, 2007	Colorado Board of Dental Examiners (Lone Tree, CO)	0
Dec. 05, 2007	Memorial Blood Centers (Duluth, MN)	268,000
Dec. 01, 2007	Community Blood Center/Battelle & Battelle LLC (Oakwood, OH)	600
Nov.30, 2007	Prescription Advantage (MA)	150,000
Nov. 29, 2007	American Red Cross(North Dallas)	0
Nov. 21, 2007	United Healthcare (New York, NY)	0
Nov. 17, 2007	Ohio Masonic Home / Battelle & Battelle LLC (Springfield, OH	600
Nov 15, 2007	Roudebush VA Medical Center (Indianapolis, IN)	12,000
Nov. 07, 2007	Carolinas Medical Center – NorthEast (Concord, NC)	28,000
Nov. 05, 2007	Alabama Department of Public Health (Montgomery, AL)	1,554
Oct. 30, 2007	Pathology Group (Memphis, TN)	75,000
Oct. 23, 2007	West Virginia Public Employees Insurance Agency (Charleston, WV)	200,000
Oct. 04, 2007	Massachusetts Division of Professional Licensure (Boston, MA)	450,000
Oct. 02, 2007	Athens Regional Health Services (Athens, GA)	1,400
Sept. 19, 2007	University of Michigan School of Nursing (Ann Arbor, MI)	8,585
Sept. 12, 2007	TennCare / Americhoice Inc. (Knoxville, TN)	67,000
Sept. 11, 2007	Pennsylvania Public Welfare Department	
	(Harrisburg, PA). Mental health histories of more than	300,000
2,000		
Sept. 09, 2007	McKesson Health-care services (San Francisco, CA)	0
Sept. 01, 2007	Johns Hopkins Hospital (Baltimore, MD)	5,783
	Total Number of Identities "Lost"	1,378,522

0 = Unknown, facility could not calculate   Source: PrivacyRights.Org

the numbers are going up every year. Now you see why the security professional in me gets nervous.

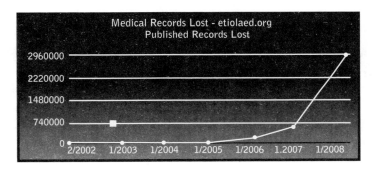

Now, most of these medical facilities will do the right thing and give you a free credit watch for a year. Big deal! My identity in exchange for a $29.95 credit watch? You can start to protect yourself by checking the list of breaches at the web site above. How many of the companies are you currently doing business with?

Wasn't HIPAA supposed to fix these problems?

The Health Insurance Portability and Accountability Act (HIPAA) was passed to help protect our medical information. Did you notice portability was more important than accountability? Ask anybody in the medical field and they start swearing about – cursing - the law.

I tell facilities that if they want to get HIPAA-compliant fast, go hire two IT professionals from a bank. They'll walk in, see how bad the security is, and freak out. Give them two months and enough? money - poof, you're compliant. When you look at the entire alphabet soup of security laws (FIS-

MA, GLBA, SOx, FIRPA, PCI-DSS, 17799-2005), HIPAA ranks among the lowest in terms of its requirements. This act was only the minimum security recommended. Thus the freak-out by bank IT professionals.

We can see how successful HIPAA has been in preventing medical identity theft by looking at how many medical facilities have been breached from year to year. If HIPAA was doing what it was supposed to do (preventing breaches), then the number of breaches would be going down. Unfortunately, since HIPAA's inception in 2003, medical facility breaches continue to go up every year.

Just announced in 2007 is the fact the people who run HIPAA are now going to audit hospitals that have been found guilty of a HIPAA violation. Now, this is a totally new development because, in the past, if you had a complaint filed against your organization (over 4,000 so far) or had already been proven to be in violation (200 so far), very little occurred beyond the complaint (the Feds provided you with a stern talking to). Price Cooper Waterhouse has been selected to conduct audits of facilities that have had a proven violation against them.

While this is a start, the problem is that this step is coming years too late, and HIPAA will only be doing audits on "10 or 20" facilities out of the entire list of organizations that have had violations. Does this appear to be the work of an organization that wants to protect YOUR identity?!

Another way to gauge the effectiveness of HIPAA is to see how many people have been prosecuted according to this law designed to protect medical data. The number of people who've been prosecuted under the law indicate the (lack of) consideration that HIPAA gives to medical identity theft. To date only 5 people have been prosecuted for HIPAA violations. These people were selling patients' data to others!

Doesn't the average worker feel responsible for protecting my record?

So the bad news thus far is that hospitals lose medical records full of data. The law designed to prevent this and protect your information has no teeth and the hospitals ignore it. But how serious is the average health worker about your data? Most are very caring people who do anything to get the patient better. Overworked and underpaid, they get their impression of HIPAA from the medical facility and we know the medical facility doesn't embrace its purpose. In October 2007 patient medical records and patient privacy got lots of media attention because Hollywood movie star George Clooney apparently had his medical records violated by employees at the Palisades Medical Center in New Jersey. They allegedly shared his medical records with the news media. Clooney was admitted to this facility when he and girlfriend, Sarah Larson, were treated for injuries sustained in a motorcycle accident recently. The Clooney incident speaks volumes about how health workers value your information.

"None of the employees, each suspended for four weeks, were doctors treating Clooney, administrators said, raising a host of questions about who can view private medical information and what measures are in place to protect patients' privacy," ABC news reported.

OK, everybody who peeked at the records had been through HIPAA classes; they all signed a statement acknowledging they understood. Yet, they all looked. Hey, would you like to buy Clooney's birth date, his mother's maiden name and his bank account numbers? All these were contained on his "protected" medical record.

Even the facility's security guard had access to Clooney's records. What need does the guard have to look at medical or financial record of patients!? Maybe a list of patients, but going beyond that reflects a lack of network security. That's just bad network design.

What can YOU do about Medical Identity Theft?

Start by realizing there is a problem with medical records being "lost" by facilities. This awareness is hard for some people to come to because of the pedestal we put people in the health field on. We want to believe they are doing their best to help and protect us and our records while we're in their care.

Second, educate yourself on ways of protecting your identity. Identity theft has now become a "when" not an "if." Be proactive in protecting yourself, so when some link slips on the chain of medical care, you'll be ready.

I'm proud of you already because you're reading this book. It shows you're serious about protecting yourself and your family from medical identity theft when it comes knocking on your hospital room door. Thanks.

Brad Smith, Director, Computer Institute of the Rockies

Brad Smith (RN, ASCIE, BS-Psy MCNPS, CISSP, NSA-IAM) started his computer training in 1971 and is still going strong. In 1996 his software "2the BedSide" was a national Microsoft / HIMSS spotlight software winner. His company, the Computer Institute of the Rockies was selected as the 2005 Microsoft Small Business Solution Partner of the Year for their innovative and cost effective business solutions.

Currently, Brad is a private practice informatics nurse, helping rural and frontier medical facilities comply with the complex HIPAA requirements. He believes security can be increased without impeding health care. Brad was the first Registered Nurse (RN) and Certified Information System Security Professional (CISSP) in America.

3. Character identity theft

"GEORGETOWN, GA.--As hard as it was to spend 35 years in prison for stealing a black-and-white television, Junior Allen has found freedom in many ways just as frustrating.

Despite extensive prison records in North Carolina, where he has spent more than half his life as inmate No. 0004604, Allen has been unable to establish his identity in rural Georgia, where he now lives with his sister, or in Alabama, where he was born 65 years ago to sharecropper parents.

The month long effort to get a birth certificate and photo ID only hint at the new challenge he faces -- that of transforming himself from less-than-model inmate to average senior citizen.

"It's like I never existed," Allen said. "I went to Columbus, Georgia, and they said I had to go to Alabama. I went to Alabama and they said I had to go to Georgia."

His most immediate goal is to get a driver's license."

"Ex-inmate frustrated by freedom,
Man who served time for TV theft can't get identity,"
Charleston Post and Courier

Your integrity depends on the public record of your past behavior. If you've stayed fairly clean most of your life, are a reasonably responsible person, and have managed your finances more or less well, your opportunities in life are better than if there is a fat dossier at the local police station and in the FBI files. So what does this have to do with identity theft?

It has everything in the world to do with ID theft!

Remember the title of our previous book – "Who is You?" This was much more than a clever title. It is a description of the "back end" dynamics that determine the "front end" persona people know.

You are basically what the countless data bases say you are. These data bases are comprised of your birth data, educational record, past residency, criminal activity, and financial behavior. That's fine except that your **actual record** and one or more parallel records that impersonate you may have no relationship to each other. Never mind stolen credit cards that require you to cancel the card, have the company swallow the illegitimate overages (most illegal charges on your stolen card will be absorbed by the company), and get new cards. The real horror story comes when your name, social security number, and "person" is stolen by someone who commits crimes and mayhem.

Since you are probably living in your apartment, condo, or home minding your own business, the authorities will undoubtedly find YOU when they go on the hunt for your "identity clone." Suddenly you find yourself arrested, handcuffed, and hauled to jail. Or you are issued a subpoena charging you with things you've never heard of in places you've never been. How do you PROVE that you have never been there, done that? After all, "your" name, "your" Social Security number, "your" credit cards, "your" signature, "your" driver's license are all identified with the crimes.

There was a fascinating article recently about how "facts" linger on the Internet far, far past the time when something occurred. For example, if during "your" (clone's) crime spree, stories appeared in newspapers all over the country or world with your name as the culprit, even after you have cleared your name with authorities and been released from prison, the stories of "your" crimes will continue to pop up on a Google or Lexis-Nexus search forever! When an employer or anyone else searches the Net, you will reappear day after day, month after month, as a criminal. It will take years to remove this information and you will probably never be fully restored.

4. Synthetic identity theft

The fourth and latest form of ID theft is called Synthetic ID fraud where the identity is fabricated rather than stolen. Synthetic identity fraud comprises 88.3 percent of all identity fraud events and 73.8 percent of the total dollars lost by U.S. businesses.

It is easy to see how crooks manage to create these synthetic persons. A data tape containing information on 650,000 retail customers vanished from a business called the Iron Mountain data storage company. The missing tape contains personal information from customers of J.C. Penney and 100 other retailers, including 150,000 Social Security numbers. No one seems to know where the tape went but the company, as is always the case, said there was no evidence that the information from these tapes had been used to commit any crimes or identity theft.

A 2007 report by the Government Accountability Office (GAO) found that law enforcement agencies often could not track cases of identity theft back to data breaches because the fraud did not occur until a year or more after the loss or theft of the information.

It is also important to note how extensive data losses have become and therefore how much confidential information is floating out there for criminals to use in creating fake identities. According to the watchdog group Identity Theft Resource Center's 2007 data breach report, there were 448 data breaches in 2007, exposing over 127 million personal information records to potential identity theft or fraud.

--Jan. 20, 2008 http://www.consumeraffairs.com

Financial hardship, medical privacy breaches, and character assassination are like the three horsemen and now you can add synthetic identity theft to your personal Apocalypse. They will make your life hell, will cause you to go into anxiety and depression, and can easily ruin your life. In a few cases it has already caused such pain that people have committed suicide.

Identity theft is not a minor crime.

Since in some cases it can cause death, maybe it should be a capital offense. In the meantime, consumers do have one excellent recourse and that is to use professional services such as some form of effective identity theft monitoring service to alert them of any suspicious activities using their Social Security number, name, and other personal information.

Victims Can Suffer More Than Financial Harm. Individuals may need to spend substantial amounts of time contacting creditors, establishing that they were not responsible for the identity thief's fraudulent transactions and purchases, and getting their credit histories and financial records corrected. Criminals committing identity theft can harm reputations, create greater stress in family life and other relationships, and, on occasion, cause the unwarranted arrest of a victim whose name is being used by the identity thief.

 - Fact Sheet: The President's Identity Theft Task Force

It should be pretty obvious from the review of ID theft and loss above, that the old advice of "be careful with your information, make sure you shred all sensitive information," etc. is good advice but is absolutely worthless if someone who owns and manages your vital data loses that information! Those who argue that consumers don't need an identity theft protection service and can take care of the consequences of ID theft themselves would probably also argue that consumers don't need collision or personal injury insurance on their vehicle because they can self-insure and set aside money in a savings account. That too is naïve advice.

The Rest of the Case

 United States Attorney David E. Nahmias
 Northern District of Georgia
 FOR IMMEDIATE RELEASE CONTACT:
 Patrick Crosby
 11/16/07 (404) 581-6016
 http://www.usdoj.gov/usao/gan/ FAX (404) 581-6160

MATTHEW COX SENTENCED TO OVER 26 YEARS IN PRISON FOR ATLANTA, NASHVILLE, AND TAMPA MORTGAGE FRAUDS

Former Fugitive Sentenced For Using Dozens Of Stolen Identities, Including Those Of Minor Children And The Homeless, To Commit Mortgage Fraud In 8 States

Atlanta, GA - MATTHEW BEVAN COX, 38, formerly of Nashville, Atlanta, and Tampa, was sentenced today by United States District Judge Timothy C. Batten, Sr., on charges of mortgage fraud, identity theft, passport fraud and violation of the terms of his probation.

"Cox will now be serving the long prison sentence he deserves for his crimes," said United States Attorney David E. Nahmias in Atlanta. "While the subject of a nationwide manhunt, Cox repeatedly used the stolen identities of minor children, the homeless and others to place multiple fraudulent loans on the same property without the knowledge or consent of the true owners. His crimes resulted in clouded property titles in several states with years of unresolved litigation, a trail of over 100 victims, and millions of dollars in losses that cannot be recovered."

"The Secret Service has taken an aggressive stance in the prevention and investigation of mortgage fraud and other forms of identity theft", said James Byers, Special Agent in Charge of the United States Secret Service Atlanta Field Office. "This case shows both the wide-reaching effects of identity crimes as well as the importance of cooperation among law enforcement to focus resources and respond effectively to uncover and prevent this type of financial fraud."

COX was sentenced to 26 years, 4 months in prison to be followed by 5 years of supervised release and was ordered to pay $5,975,900 in restitution. The court also ordered a forfeiture judgment of $6,000,000 in assets. COX pleaded guilty to these charges on April 10, 2007.

According to United States Attorney Nahmias and the information presented in court: COX rented or agreed to purchase properties from true owners, fraudulently erased prior mortgage liens and assumed the identity of the owners, and used a stolen identity or paid straw borrowers to obtain multiple mortgage loans on the same property. COX then changed locations and committed similar mortgage fraud schemes in other states. COX and his co-conspirators used stolen identities to execute the mortgage fraud, including identities of minor children and those he received from conducting what he termed "Federal Surveys" of homeless and drug rehab patients. COX also used these stolen identities to obtain drivers' licenses and state identification cards, purchase vehicles, lease mail drops and virtual offices, rent apartments, open bank accounts and apply for credit cards, birth certificates and a passport used for travel to Jamaica, Italy, Greece and other foreign destinations while a federal fugitive.

(NEWS MEDIA NOTE: Within the next week, up to four paintings made by COX will be auctioned on the eBay Internet service, with all proceeds to be directly given to victims. News media are encouraged to include the auction in coverage of the case which may result in increased restitution to the mortgage fraud victims in three states.)

This case was investigated by Special Agents of the United States Secret Service. The investigation of co-defendants in this case continues by Special Agents of the Federal Bureau of Investigation. Assistant United States Attorney Gale McKenzie prosecuted the case. For further information please contact David E. Nahmias (pronounced NAH-me-us), United States Attorney, or Charysse L. Alexander, Executive Assistant United States Attorney, through Patrick Crosby,

Public Affairs Officer, U.S. Attorney's Office, at (404) 581-6016. The Internet address for the HomePage for the U.S. Attorney's Office for the Northern District of Georgia is www.usdoj.gov/usao/gan.

In Chapter 4 we will teach you the lingo of ID theft. We feel that it is very useful for you to know the particulars of "Nigerian Scam" or what "Phishing and Pharming" is so that you become more aware and can have more intelligent conversations on these topics.

CHAPTER 4

ENDLESS SCAMS

Scams succeed because of two things. Firstly, a scam looks like the real thing. It appears to meet your need or desire. To find out that it is in fact a scam, you must first make the effort to check it properly. You need to ask questions and think carefully before you decide what to do. Depending on the issue, you could do that on the spot, or you might need help – and that could take several days. This website will help you with that process.

Secondly, scammers manipulate you by 'pushing your buttons' to produce the automatic response they want. It's nothing to do with you personally; it's to do with the way individuals in society are wired up emotionally and socially. It's because the response is automatic that people fall for the scam.

http://www.scamwatch.gov.au/content/scams/succeed.asp

How many identity theft scams are there?

Let us count the ways.

The E-Bay e-mail was urgent. "Your account has been compromised. In order to secure your E-Bay account we are asking you to verify your password and change it so that you can continue to enjoy E-Bay services. If you do not respond, your account will be blocked. Please click on the link in this e-mail and follow the instructions"

You may say "Yikes! I don't want my E-Bay privileges cancelled! How am I going to get rid of all those porcelain Elvis coasters I've been picking up at garage sales?!"

In our case all this was no problem. We have never bought or sold anything on E-Bay. We don't have an account. We clicked the delete button – there were FIVE simultaneous messages like this, which in itself gave away the spam fraud. Oh, incidentally, we also don't have any Elvis coasters!

So, number one, scams are e-mail phishing (fishing) expeditions asking unsuspecting Internet and e-mail users to update their accounts, confirm their accounts, passwords, credit card numbers and PINs, and a host of other tricks for prying confidential information from you. Your e-mail has been compiled into dozens of mailing lists that are sold on the Internet to anyone who wants to buy them. The reason it's called phishing is that the junk sellers, ("PENIS ENLARGE-MENT- Guaranteed", "genuine Viagra for 10 cents a pill!"), or ID thieves throw in the e-mail "hooks" and figger that if they send out, say a billion messages (yes, one phisher sent out over one billion spam e-mails!) a few suckers will bite the hook. Spam e-mail is

"... unsolicited e-mail on the Internet. From the sender's point-of-view, it's a form of bulk mail, often to a list culled from subscribers to a Usenet discussion group or obtained by companies that specialize in creating e-mail distribution lists. To the receiver, it usually seems like junk e-mail. In general, it's not considered good netiquette to send spam. It's generally equivalent to unsolicited phone marketing calls except that the user pays for part of the message since everyone shares the cost of maintaining the Internet." http:// www.google.com/search?hl=en&lr=&oi=defmore&q=defi ne:Spam

Like "junk mail" that used to come in your analog mailbox, this attack against your sanity and personal identity security has exploded parallel to the growth of e-mail as a medium of communication. So you are pestered and your daily work is plagued by unwanted messages. You may end up buying sugar pills instead of Viagra (you'll notice that soon!), or a cheap cruise ship vacation – we got one for $200 from Miami to Nassau for 3 days! – that is fake. In this case we say "buyer beware" because if it sounds WAY too good to be true, it is.

But, the difference between this junk mail and the ones that come in an envelope is that at the click of your mouse, you may reveal information that you would rarely if ever write on a form, attach a stamp to, and mail back to the "analog" crooks of the past. (Side bar – even in the old days many, many people actually did fall for endless identity or money schemes, and did mail back the information, and lost money and precious privacy). What's really different is the massive scope of e-fraud and the speed as well as volume with which it is committed.

The experts tell us that legitimate businesses rarely if ever e-mail critically important information to you although, of course, many people do their banking on-line and never step into a brick and mortar bank and have therefore become numbed and think that e- commerce is normal and safe.

There are, however, cases. The security firm McAfee apparently sent out an e-mail on June 13, 2005 asking subscribers of expiring web-based virus protection to visit their web site, click on a link, and provide a credit card number to renew the subscription. (Business Week, July 18,2005, p. 16). Nowadays this can be a very risky move since thieves have become very good at emulating real web sites of legitimate companies or organizations. The problem is that people actually like to do business instantly on the web especially for software applications that can be updated by a quick download. Shopping on the web, on e-bay, buying books or other gifts, which are delivered efficiently, has also become huge. So there is a classic approach-avoidance conflict for most people.

Even we, as authors of a book entitled **Identity Theft** have taken the chance!

We were working recently at a site where there was high-speed wireless Internet access. We needed Internet access and logged on to the service site for a short term, three-day subscription. The service was recommended to us but when we looked at the sign-up form, we realized that it was not a "secure" site, which uses encryption and other security features. (https://www.anonsecuresite.com is a secure site – the http has an "s" at the end – whereas http://www.anonse-curesite.com is not – there is no "s" after http!). So why did we take a chance? First, we needed access and this was the only provider. Second, we used a limited amount credit card, which, even if someone got the number, would only have a small amount of authorized cash. In fact, we suggest that you get one of these cards to use for Internet and e-commerce purchases.

Other common Internet identity and monetary scams include:

• In 1588 there was the 'Spanish Prisoner' scam. The alleged prisoner was shackled in a Spanish castle dungeon and required money to bribe the jailers to be released. The letters were written by the fictitious prisoner who promised a share of his treasure chest – which was rumored to be huge - in return for help. Today this is called **The Nigerian scam**, so called because when it first began was in the form of e-mails purported to be from the son, brother, wife, or cabinet-minister of the "former president of Nigeria" who has a bank account with over $50 million in deposits in a Swiss bank. To free these funds we must provide a guaranteed deposit to the bank of $30,000 US dollars. "I am prepared to share 10 million with you if you will provide the withdrawal funding." The e-mail usually says something like, "your name was provided to me by a close mutual friend who has told me you are an honorable person who has an impeccable reputation and will honor my request for complete confidentiality in this matter." These letters still come to our e-mail in-box now from all over the world!

•   **The lottery winner scam** which says that you have already won the Irish lottery or some other game of chance, tells you how much money you won, and asks you to go to the web site or open an attachment to claim your winnings.

We have never bitten the hook of these phishing expeditions, but the industry is clear that they are all scams – your money will be taken and if you click on links, you may be in even deeper trouble because a piece of malicious software (malware) may be dropped on your computer with unknown but always negative consequences.

It's one thing to answer an e-mail and willingly yield your most precious confidential information. It's another when you play no role whatsoever in the heist!

Just yesterday we were doing some work on the Internet and had looked up some information we needed for a presentation and a radio interview. Suddenly a window popped up and asked what we wanted to do with a file – install it, delete it, or close it?

We had not opened any attachment from an e-mail. We had not even received an e-mail with an attachment. We looked at the name on the pop up and it was an ".exe" file.

We have learned that with rare exceptions normally when you are deliberately asked for an application to install on your computer, you should not install. Delete and never, EVER install an .exe file unless you know exactly what you are installing.

In a new and nefarious technique, dangerous installations can now be delivered to your computer from just being connected to the Internet or from opening your browser without ever clicking on anything, and without opening any files.

This is, of course, only one of a host of dangerous passive or invisible threats to your privacy, your security, and therefore your sanity. The following terms are good to remember because knowing about these is essential for safe computing.

Bluesnarfing – This is the theft of information from a wireless device through a Bluetooth connection. "Bluetooth is a high-speed but very short-range wireless technology for exchanging data between desktop and mobile computers, personal digital assistants (PDAs), and other devices. By exploiting vulnerability in the way Bluetooth is implemented on a mobile phone, an attacker can access information -- such as the user's calendar, contact list and e-mail and text messages -- without leaving any evidence of the attack. Other devices that use Bluetooth, such as laptop computers, may also be vulnerable ..." http://searchmobilecomputing. techtarget.com/sDefinition/0,,sid40_gci952393,00.html

Greyware n.) a new term – in the tech world new terms are invented on an hourly or daily basis! This refers to "a malicious software or code that is considered to fall in the "grey area" between normal software and a virus. Greyware is a term which all other malicious or annoying software such as adware, spyware, trackware, and other malicious code and malicious shareware fall under." http://www.webopedia. com/TERM/G/greyware.html

These are only a few of the scams and the tools used to mine information that can then easily be used to do personal and financial damage to the legitimate owner of the information.

Although we have a separate section on Social Security numbers, we want to make a few comments on that crucially important ID number in this chapter.

Every American citizen or resident is issued a Social Security number. Although groups like the American Civil Liberties Union are in denial about this, the SS # is the American national identity number. It has been used to identify you from birth to death; it has been used as the official student ID number at all levels of education; it was once the number put on state drivers' licenses, and many people still print their Social Security number on their checks! Until recently I had to write the number on a form and fax it to the Instructional Technology office at my university in order to get a key to the media station in my classroom. These forms were filed somewhere not very secure and could be accessed by anyone interested in checking them out.

Lax and extensive use of this number allowed people to use the number and personal information on the person associated with that number, to apply for credit cards, passports, drivers' licenses, and all manner of other stuff. We are now becoming more possessive about revealing this magic number. Drivers' licenses for the most part don't use the number anymore and many colleges and schools have devised their own distinct student ID numbers.

However a friend recently went clothing shopping. At the chain called The PAZz she found pants, a belt, and three shirts on sale. When she was ready to check out, the clerk said, "If you get a PAZz credit card, you'll get a 20% discount." My friend said, "Sure, why not" and filled out the application. Besides the name and address, the form required her Social Security number, which she dutifully filled in. Why the SS number? Because it is the root verifier of identity for getting a credit check from one of the three big, national credit services that are the "Gods" of your financial worthiness.

When she told me about this, I suddenly realized that in addition to the virtual and remote scams that can steal your person and your identity through the Internet, one of the weak links in our protection is any store that issues credit cards. An ID theft ring just has to place a member or a stringer in a major store and when the application forms are filled out, snap a digital picture and ship these .jpg files to "scam central." There are now 5 megapixel cameras the size of a credit card! So, credit card applications are surely a juicy and very widespread security breach.

Of course, we all know that credit scammers also can do their evil deeds in restaurants where wait-staff can be equipped with pocket size swipers into which they can enter all the information on the magnetic strip of your card. This information can then be taken home, dumped, read, and used to steal your credit card and even your wider identity. The magnetic strip on your card contains a lot more information than just your credit card number and expiration date!

Incidentally, as we mentioned earlier, when you check out of that hotel you should NEVER leave the key card (the one you swipe or insert into your door to open your room lock) lying on the bedside table in your room! It turns out that the magnetic strip on the card (some don't have a strip just a bunch of holes that correspond to your lock and those are harmless) usually has a lot more information than just the combination for your room. It may have your name, address, phone number, credit card number, and a host of other information. ALWAYS return the magnetic room key to the front desk where the card will be recycled and your information erased for the next guest.

Ok, now that you've been drilled on the basic horror stories of scams, let's just finish with a few more super stories!

If you want a truly hair-raising experience on hacking and insecurity go to "BigByte Technologies" web site. http://www.bigbytetech.ca/

Here you will find a long list of intrusions of all sorts that can put your identity at risk. These are updated on a daily basis and provide a trail of tears for the enormous dangers posed by the Internet and by Information technologies.

Here is a sampling of some of the interesting problems.

The first deals with truly cruel exploitation of tragedies when people go to the Internet for information.

A virus has been spotted in the wild, which attempts to exploit concerns surrounding the bomb blasts that rocked London last Thursday and left at least 50 people dead. An e-mail purporting to offer a link to amateur video footage of the events on the London Underground in the aftermath of the bomb blast will install a Trojan on users' machines if they click on the attachment. According to UK e-mail security firm MessageLabs the e-mail appears as a mocked-up html newsletter from CNN with the subject line 'TERROR HITS LONDON'. The sender's e-mail address appears as breakingnews@CNNonline.com. Although that address could easily have been spoofed, the domain is not an official CNN domain and is registered to a firm in Florida. The e-mail asks recipients to 'See attachments for unique amateur video shots'. **"Virus writer exploits London bomb blast,"**

July 11, 2005, http://www.optusnet.com.au

If you clicked on this link, a virus (Trojan horse) was then downloaded to your computer and executed. This virus then allowed the thugs who sent it to use your computer to send spam e-mail and presumably use your computer for other potential criminal activity.

According to the tech community, the same thing happened when the tsunami hit the Indian Ocean, when the war in Iraq unfolded, and also after the 9/11 terrorist attacks. (Reported by several on-line sites- the best review from CNET).

Another issue covered deals with the convenient but notoriously unsafe wireless Internet access.

*[Benjamin Smith III] faces a pretrial hearing this month following his arrest for what some tech-savvy kids call a "Wi-Fi drive-by" and others call "war-driving" or "wacking" (Web hacking) ... Smith was charged under a Florida law barring unauthorized access to computer networks after a resident named Richard Dinon caught him sitting in a SUV with a laptop, allegedly tapping into Dinon's wireless home computer network using a technology called wireless fidelity [Wi-Fi]. Drive-by means that somebody pulls up to the curb or into the alley and taps into your wireless Internet account right alongside your own computers. **Wi-Fi hackers find routes easily; path tough to block**, by James Coates, Chicago Tribune, reported in the Los Angeles times, July 10, 2005.*

Wireless Internet access is a wonderful way to use your laptop and a convenience that is spreading like wildfire. People can buy the boxes to set up a wireless network in their office or home. The reason why people can penetrate this is that default settings from the factory and the lame generic user names and passwords that come with these, make it a cinch for half-smart hackers to break in. Once they access the wireless hot spot, many hackers find that they can access all of the files on the computer because the file sharing and security setting on the computer is often set for easy access to all the files.

The point that's made by wireless experts is that there are ways to make Wi-Fi networks secure, but the truth is also that for most "civilians" (ordinary computer users), it is virtually impossible to do this properly (and without screwing up everything else and shutting yourself out of the computer to boot!). In fact, we had one of the real national Wi-Fi security experts set up a wireless enhancement on our boat so that it could pick up an iffy signal from the Wi-Fi network in the marina. After at least two hours and a mind-boggling amount of clicking, number entering, IP address checking, grumbling and an occasional curse, he got it all set up!

Clearly, Wi-Fi is another example of an industry that is clueless about usability for its customers. It should be just as easy to set up and secure a Wi-Fi network at home or office as locking a gate. The lack of common sense, intuitive and plug-and-play ways of managing computers is an invitation for people to leave their systems vulnerable ("At least it's working!" a friend of ours sighed).

Even James Coates, tech writer for the Chicago Tribune (see above) wrote that

Beyond passwords, the routers accept extremely powerful encryption keys that approach the bulletproof level of na-

tional security agencies. The D-Link set-up software makes this so-called DES encryption available but offers no help beyond a cryptic message that keys must be entered as hexa-decimal numbers made up of A through F and 0 through 9. When I tried to set up just the password, the software would accept one but then wouldn't take the same password the next time. But by leaving the password and encryption blank--like a fool--the software worked fine, broadcasting my network as "default" and permitting logons as "admin." So I guess this leaves me with little more to say than what a lot of other folks are saying to the lurking Wi-Fi drive-by hackers: "Come on in; the surfing's free and it's on me."

This of course is a completely unacceptable condition under the best of circumstances but certainly intolerable given the rapid rise of malicious and often criminal intrusions into people's computer systems and the sharp rise in crime and identity theft.

When Companies Behave Badly

"The FTC alleged that the company stored credit card information indefinitely on computers, without using proper encryption software or access controls. As a result, the FTC alleges that a hacker was able to attack Life is Good's Web site to access credit card numbers, expiration dates, and security codes of thousands of customers. The settlement bars Life is Good from making deceptive claims about its privacy and security policies, as well as have an independent auditor assess its security program on a biennial basis for the next 20 years."

The Boston Business Journal, Thursday, January 17, 2008

If you go to the shopping site "the company" referred to above http://www.lifeisgood.com/, you will see a cheerful colorful site and smiling people. There are all kinds of links to their products and all is well in cyber-shopping land. You would never guess nor does the company inform its customers that they were very sloppy with their customer's security. Strangely enough you have probably never heard of this case or the company.

The truth of the matter is that the news media treats most identity theft cases as uninteresting and simply won't report them. It takes an extraordinary and HUGE problem before most media will report it. The Boston Business Journal was the only hit we got in a general Google search of this case. We had to go to the Federal Trade Commission for the full details.

Our editors felt that it was very important to share the **full story** with you since many of you are business owners or managers and since, certainly ALL of you have shopped on line.

For those of you who work for companies or other organizations that collect sensitive private information, the lesson is very clear – that data MUST be secured in such a way that it is safe from attack and criminal abuse. For those of you who shop online be warned that your identity information is in the hands of many companies who have no idea and couldn't care less how to secure your identity.

This brings us back to the points made earlier about the need for aggressive implementation of identity theft regulations, constant and widespread training of company executives regarding their responsibility as they conduct business, run colleges, manage hospitals and clinics, or build data bases of insurance customers.

It would be interesting to know if any of the customers of Life is Good had identity theft insurance because clearly they would have been notified early by their underwriter of any suspicious use of the their credit and they would have started fixing their losses quickly.

Here is a headline you don't want to see, especially if you've been shopping for clothes lately - "Online Apparel Retailer Settles FTC Charges That It Failed to Safeguard Consumers' Sensitive Information, in Violation of Federal Law: Credit Card Numbers, Expiration Dates and Security Codes of Thousands of Consumers Compromised."

What follows is the official FTC press release on this issue.

"An apparel company that collected sensitive consumer information and pledged to keep it secure has agreed to settle Federal Trade Commission charges that its security claims were deceptive and violated federal law. The order against Life is good, Inc. and Life is good Retail, Inc. bars deceptive claims about privacy and security policies and requires that the companies implement a comprehensive information-security program and obtain audits by an independent third-party security professional every other year for 20 years.

Life is good designs and sells retail apparel and accessories and operates the Web site, www.lifeisgood.com. According to the FTC's complaint, through its Web site, Life is good has collected sensitive consumer information, including names, addresses, credit card numbers, credit card expiration dates, and credit card security codes. Its privacy policy claimed, "We are committed to maintaining our customers' privacy. We collect and store information you share with us - name, address, credit card and phone numbers along with information about products and services you request. All information is kept in a secure file and is used to tailor our communications with you." Contrary to these claims, the FTC alleges that Life is good failed to provide reasonable and appropriate security for the sensitive consumer information stored on its computer network. Specifically, the FTC charged that the company:

• unnecessarily risked credit card information by storing it indefinitely in clear, readable text on its network, and by storing credit security card codes;

• failed to assess adequately the vulnerability of its Web site and corporate computer network to commonly known and reasonably foreseeable attacks, such as SQL injection attacks;

• failed to implement simple, free or low-cost, and readily available security defenses to SQL and similar attacks; failed to use readily available security measures to monitor and control connections from the network to the Internet; and

• failed to employ reasonable measures to detect unauthorized access to credit card information.

The FTC alleges that, as a result of these failures, a hacker was able to use SQL injection attacks on Life is good's Web site to access the credit card numbers, expiration dates, and security codes of thousands of consumers.

The settlement bars Life is good from making deceptive claims about its privacy and security policies. It requires the company to establish and maintain a comprehensive security program reasonably designed to protect the security, confidentiality, and integrity of personal information it collects from consumers. The program must contain administrative, technical, and physical safeguards appropriate to Life is good's size, the nature of its activities, and the sensitivity of the personal information it collects. Specifically, Life is good must:

• Designate an employee or employees to coordinate the information security program.

• Identify internal and external risks to the security and confidentiality of personal information and assess the safeguards already in place.

• Design and implement safeguards to control the risks identified in the risk assessment and monitor their effectiveness.

• Develop reasonable steps to select and oversee service providers that handle the personal information of Life is good customers.

• Evaluate and adjust its information-security program to reflect the results of monitoring, any material changes to the company's operations, or other circumstances that may impact the effectiveness of its security program.

The settlement requires Life is good to retain an independent, third party security auditor to assess its security program on a biennial basis for the next 20 years. The auditor will be required to certify that Life is good's security program meets or exceeds the requirements of the FTC's order and is operating with sufficient effectiveness to provide reasonable assurance that the security of consumers' personal information is being protected.

The settlement also contains bookkeeping and record keeping provisions to allow the agency to monitor compliance with its order.

The Commission vote to accept the proposed consent agreement was 5-0. The FTC will publish an announcement regarding the agreement in the Federal Register shortly. The agreement will be subject to public comment for 30 days, beginning today and continuing through February 18, after which the Commission will decide whether to make it final. Comments should be addressed to the FTC, Office of the Secretary, Room H-135, 600 Pennsylvania Avenue, N.W., Washington, D.C. 20580. The FTC is requesting that any comment filed in paper form near the end of the public comment period be sent by courier or overnight service, if possible, because U.S. postal mail in the Washington area and at the Commission is subject to delay due to heightened security precautions.

Copies of the complaint, proposed consent agreement, and an analysis of the agreement to aid in public comment are available from the FTC's Web site at **http://www.ftc. gov** and also from the FTC's Consumer Response Center, Room 130, 600 Pennsylvania Avenue, N.W., Washington, D.C. 20580.

The FTC works for the consumer to prevent fraudulent, deceptive, and unfair business practices and to provide information to help spot, stop, and avoid them. To file a complaint in English or Spanish, click http://**www.ftc.gov/ftc/ complaint.shtm** or call 1-877-382-4357. The FTC enters Internet, telemarketing, identity theft, and other fraud-related complaints into Consumer Sentinel, a secure, online database available to more than 1,600 civil and criminal law enforcement agencies in the U.S. and abroad. For free information on a variety of consumer topics, click **http://ftc.gov/bcp/consumer.shtm.**

For Release: January 17, 2007
MEDIA CONTACT:
Claudia Bourne Farrell
Office of Public Affairs
202-326-2181

This example drills down into one company that was sloppy and negligent with ID information. In Chapter 5 we will lay out the specific responsibilities that businesses must assume when they collect and use sensitive customer information. We should make it very clear that insurance companies in particular must lock down and secure the personal information of their customers since they have a very special ethical and legal responsibility.

CHAPTER 5

CORPORATE AND BUSINESS OBLIGATIONS

"If you experience a security breach, 20% of your affected customer base will no longer do business with you, 40% will consider ending the relationship, and 5% will be hiring lawyers! When it comes to cleaning up the mess, companies on average spend 1,600 work hours per incident at a cost of $40,000 to $92,000 per victim."

CIO Magazine, The Coming Pandemic, May 15, 2006

Nearly every company in the United States and Canada collects and stores sensitive non-public information (NPI) about customers on its computers - information such as names, addresses, Social Security numbers, credit card numbers, and account numbers that specifically identify the customer or their own employees. It is this information that you as a business owner must protect as if it meant life or death (in this case literally the life or death of your business.) In

Chapter 8 we will cover specific laws in more detail.

It is widely understood that NPI is often needed to conduct business, payroll obligations, and streamline orders. Let's not forget it is we the consumers that demand service and product immediately. The only problem is if, in the corporate rush to satisfy the consumers' demands, the business happens to "misplace" this sensitive data or God forbid have it stolen, it can lead to devastating consequences. The cost of a data breach or security breach doesn't only amount to losing the trust of your customers, it can and will amount to thousands of dollars in fines along with huge class action lawsuits, not to mention that it is just good business practice to keep your clients' NPI secure. The following case is one example of such a loss.

A group of Michigan employees recently broke new legal ground when a jury awarded them $275,000 for the disasters that befell their lives when their union neglected to safeguard their Social Security and driver's license numbers. The verdict against Michigan Council 25 of the American Federation of State, County, and Municipal Employees (AFSCME) is the first in the nation to find that a custodian of employee information has a duty to guard the data with scrupulous care.

http://www.shrm.org   05/02/05

As security breaches increase around the world and the number of individuals affected by such breaches increases, so will the class-action lawsuits. With this case and the groundbreaking case of United States –vs.- ChoicePoint covered in detail in another chapter, precedent has been set and the groundwork laid for future lawsuits. The Michigan case can be used as a benchmark of what is to come for employers that fail to keep the NPI data files secure.

"The Michigan case is the first I've seen that affirms the imposition of liability on the person who negligently handled sensitive information," says attorney Philip Gordon of law firm Littler Mendelson. "It's a national precedent that opens the door to employer liability for workplace identity theft in other jurisdictions that likely will follow Michigan's example."

According to David Parker of law firm Charfoos and Christensen, who represented the Michigan employees, the Michigan situation occurred because officials of Michigan Council 25 of AFSCME allowed their union secretary, Yvonne Berry, to take work home, including lists of the Social Security numbers, dates of birth and driver's license information of emergency service operators working for the City of Detroit. Berry's daughter, Dentry Berry, gained access to the employee data at the home, went on a spending spree, and brought havoc to the lives of 13 public employees.

"When the charges started rolling in, for almost two years, these people had to spend hours of their days, every day, dealing with angry creditors," Parker said. "One person had to postpone her retirement because her credit had been trashed. Another couldn't get credit at a time when she needed it badly. Another had to deal with an angry wife who looked at the charges and was convinced that he'd set up housekeeping with a honey." The jury award compensated them for the mental anguish of trying to straighten out their credit histories.

http://www.shrm.org 05/02/05

In order to reduce the threat of data losses and their consequences the industry suggests the following as a minimal set of practices:

• Do not keep credit card information or numbers on your clients unless absolutely necessary.

• **If you must keep NPI, develop a written security plan and train ALL of your employees on a regular basis.**

• Lock all file cabinets and desk drawers that contain sensitive information, whether it's the clients', employees', or the business'.

• Practice the "Clean Desk" policy: all desks must be cleaned off at the end of the day.

• Require employees to log off their computers at the end of the day or if they are going to leave their workstations for a prolonged period of time.

• Require all employees to change their passwords regularly

• Make it mandatory for all employees to sign a non-disclosure and confidentiality form.

• Have in place an early warning system for potential identity theft incidents and offer it to employees as well as customers, i.e. an identity theft monitoring system that **includes proactive legal services.**

We admit these are only a few of the policies that should be implemented, yet they are a good first step. We would recommend that you have a proactive defense system in place. Betsy Broder assistant director of the FTC's Division of Privacy an Identity Protection states:

"Unless you're one of a few businesses that are exempt from our jurisdiction we will act against businesses that fail to protect their customer data."

ABA Connection - Jason Krause 2006

In a phone interview with Betsy Broder she reiterated to us what many have quoted her as saying, "We (the FTC) are not looking for a perfect fail safe system, we need to see that the businesses are taking 'reasonable' steps to protect their customers' data or NPI. We believe that implementing the above tips along with conferring with your legal council and consultants in the field you will be well covered when a breach or left occurs at you place."

Business Ethics

As we have seen, one of the crucial obligations of American (and soon Canadian and other) businesses is to secure and protect the vital personal identity information of its customers. There are federal laws that we cover in another chapter and there are also increasing state rules mandating business behavior such as the case of Hawaii, which we review below.

It is crucially important for companies and other entities that collect, manage, process, hold/store, and share sensitive identity information to behave in a manner that scrupulously respects the value of this information. This discussion is closely related to the topic of an "ethical corporate identity." This is a new field of inquiry for scholarship in ethics and corporate social responsibility or what has been traditionally called "business ethics." Business ethics includes a series of characteristics such as responsible behavior towards shareholders, transparency, community responsibility, respect for the environment as well as respect for the sensitive information on employees and customers in the custody of the company.

"In recent years, the issue of business ethics has garnered increased attention. Corporate research and watchdog groups such as the Ethics Resource Center and the Council on Economic Priorities point out that the number of corporations that engage in ethics training and initiate socially responsive programs has increased dramatically over the course of the past two decades, and that courses on business ethics have proliferated in America's business schools during that time as well. But observers have also noted that over that same period of time, the business world saw numerous instances of stock price pumping through corporate downsizing, punitive actions against "whistleblowers," and other practices that point to a still-prevalent emphasis on the bottom line over all other considerations in many industries."
http://www.answers.com/topic/business-ethics?cat=biz-fin

Identity information security and proper training for secure identity data management are rapidly becoming an integral part of the larger universe of corporate ethics. It is not only right but research also strongly indicates that ethics is very good business.

Even if you are not within the jurisdiction of the state of Hawaii, we feel that the following guidelines from that state's Department of Commerce and Consumer Affairs are very instructive. We suggest that you study them and try to conduct business (or if you are a consumer, expect your vendor to conduct business) according to the philosophy and principles incorporated in the Hawaiian guidelines. We feel that these are a very good beginning for a corporate ethics and responsibility initiative.

The key document you may wish to consult is called

"Identify Theft Information relating to the responsibilities of businesses that handle confidential personal information: New Hawaii Identity Theft Laws" and can be found at this web site:

> http://hawaii.gov/dcca/quicklinks/id_theft_info/laws/
> ID_Theft_Info_For_Businesses

The document starts by reminding us that ID theft is rapidly growing and constitutes a very serious and costly crime and then continues:

"Governor Linda Lingle signed into law several bills which will provide increased protection to Hawaii residents from identity theft. Several of these bills will directly impact Hawaii businesses. Act 135, Notification of Security Breaches, will require businesses and government agencies that keep confidential personal information about consumers to notify those consumers if that information has been compromised by an unauthorized disclosure; Act 136, Destruction of Personal Information, will require businesses and government agencies to take reasonable measures to protect against unauthorized access to an individual's personal information when disposing of the records they keep; and Act 137, Social Security Number Protection, will restrict businesses and government agencies from disclosing consumers' Social Security numbers to the general public. All of these bills share a common goal: to protect individuals from exposure to identity theft by imposing limitations and restrictions on the use and disclosure of personal information."

One of the key provisions of the law imposes " … new obligations on the part of Hawaii businesses to notify an individual whenever the individual's personal information that is maintained by the business has been compromised by unauthorized disclosure. The underlying policy behind the Act is that prompt notification will help potential victims to act against identity theft by initiating steps to monitor their credit reputation. In this regard, it is extremely important that any business subject to the Act's provisions undertake measures to fully comply with the law when it becomes effective on January 1, 2007."

When does an affected business have to take action? This is what the government of Hawaii requires:

First, a business has to ascertain if actual "personal information" has been compromised.

"Personal information" means an individual's first name or first initial and last name in combination with any one or more of the following data elements, when either the name or the data elements are not encrypted: social security number; driver's license number or Hawaii ID card number; or account number, credit or debit card number, access code, or password that would permit access to an individual's financial account. It does not include publicly available information that is lawfully made available to the general public from federal, state, or local government records.

Second, a company has to decide if a "security breach" has taken place. This law defines a "Security Breach" as " … an incident of unauthorized access to and acquisition of unencrypted or unredacted records or data containing "personal information" where illegal use of the personal information has occurred or is reasonably likely to occur and that creates a risk of harm to a person. Any incident of unauthorized access to and acquisition of encrypted records or data containing personal information along with the confidential process or key constitutes a security breach."

Determining if the security breach fits the requirements of the law is somewhat complicated and the firm should consult an attorney according to the guidelines of the state.

Let's say the affected company and its lawyer(s) have determined that personal information has been seriously compromised. What does the business need to do next?

The company first needs to inform the individuals who have been affected and do so without "unreasonable delay." There is an exception and that would be if a law enforcement agency " … informs the business in writing that notification may impede a criminal investigation or jeopardize national security."

The actual notice of the information loss has to be "clear and conspicuous" and needs to include information including a general description of the incident, the type of information that may have been compromised, what the business is doing to protect the information from another loss, contact information and general advice on how the victim can monitor his or her credit.

The Hawaiian law also spells out how a business notifies people whose information has been compromised, with different rules for incidents over 10,000 customers.

One important part of the Hawaiian law is the proper disposal of customer information when it is discarded. Shredding and other destructive methods are required since it is often from discarded records that ID thieves obtain vital confidential information. The law even spells out that if disposal contractors are hired to destroy these records, the company must establish the security and reliability of the contractor.

One very important piece of the Hawaiian law is the prevention of fraudulent use of a Social Security number (SSN) by attempting to restrict its use as an identifier. There are some interesting prohibited uses of Social Security numbers by a business include the following:

1. Intentionally communicate or otherwise make available to the general public an individual's entire social security number;

2. Intentionally print or imbed an individual's entire social security number on any card required for the individual to access products or services provided by the person or entity;

3. Require an individual to transmit the individual's entire social security number over the Internet, unless the connection is secure or the social security number is encrypted;

4. Require an individual to use the individual's entire social security number to access an Internet website, unless a password or unique personal identification number or other authentication device is also required to access the Internet website; and

5. Print an individual's entire Social Security number on any materials that are mailed to the individual, unless the materials are employer-to-employee communications, or where specifically requested by the individual.

Unfortunately there are many so-called "Permissible Uses of Social Security Numbers." As we review these, it becomes clear that American businesses are still very dependent on this sensitive number for many, many transactions including the following:

Use of the social security number in the following instances is permitted if the social security number is included in documents that are mailed and:

* *Are specifically requested by the individual identified by the social security number;*
* *Required by state or federal law to be on the document to be mailed;*
* *Required as part of an application or enrollment process;*
* *Used to establish, amend, or terminate an account, contract, or policy; or*
* *Used to confirm the accuracy of the social security number for the purpose of obtaining a credit report pursuant to the Fair Credit Reporting Act, as set forth, in 15 U.S.C. Section 1681(b).*

That is already an ample use of the most important ID number. Unfortunately there are still more instances in which the SSN can be legally used by businesses including the following:

... the opening of an account or the provision of or payment for a product or service authorized by an individual; The collection, use, or release of a social security number to investigate or prevent fraud; conduct background checks; conduct social or scientific research; collect a debt; obtain a credit report from or furnish data to a consumer reporting agency pursuant to the Fair Credit Reporting Act, 15 U.S.C. Sections 1681 to 1681x, as amended; undertake a permissible purpose enumerated under the federal Gramm Leach

Bliley Act, 15 U.S.C. Sections 6801 to 6809, as amended; locate an individual who is missing or due a benefit, such as a pension, insurance, or unclaimed property benefit; or locate a lost relative; A business or government agency acting pursuant to a court order, warrant, subpoena, or when otherwise required by law; A business or government agency providing the social security number to a federal, state, or local government entity including a law enforcement agency or court, or their agents or assigns; The collection, use, or release of a social security number in the course of administering a claim, benefit, or procedure relating to an individual's employment, including an individual's termination from employment, retirement from employment, injuries suffered during the course of employment, and other related claims, benefits, or procedures; The collection, use, or release of a social security number as required by state or federal law; The sharing of the social security number by business affiliates; The use of a social security number for internal verification or administrative purposes; A social security number that has been redacted; Documents or records that are recorded or required to be open to the public pursuant to the constitution or laws of the State or court rule or order.

When we examined this list, it became clear that even with a new and laudable set of ID information protection laws in Hawaii, the consumer's Social Security number is still going to be very widely used and therefore remain highly vulnerable.

We found the following provision to be sadly amusing: *"Notwithstanding the foregoing exceptions, a social security number that is permitted to be mailed may not be printed, in whole or in part, on a postcard or other mailer not requiring an envelope, or visible on the envelope or without the envelope having been opened."* Well, yes, we would agree that the number should not be printed on a post card that is not in an envelope! That is, to say the least, a minimal protection. SSN numbers printed on all kinds of documentation that is mailed inside envelopes becomes, as we have indicated in other places in this book, very vulnerable to mailbox thefts. ID thieves know what the mailings in which these precious numbers are used look like.

What if a business violates these guidelines? "Any business that violates any provision of Acts 135, 136, or 137 shall be subject to penalties to the State of Hawaii of not more than $2,500 for each violation. In addition, any business that violates any provision shall be liable to an injured party in an amount equal to the sum of any actual damages sustained." For most businesses our consultants agree, $2,500 is a very modest penalty and for some firms it may be more cost-effective to pay the fine than to put in place expensive and rigorous identity protection practices. Of course, it would benefit companies in Hawaii and elsewhere in the US as well to have their employees undergo regular and timely training programs to sensitize and prepare them to conduct themselves in a "safe risk management" professional manner.

We hope that you found this to be an interesting review of what business best practices look like in one case study. We also hope that you discerned that YOU are still highly vulnerable even under the Hawaiian law and that in the final analysis, it is in your interest to have a plan and perhaps even insurance to protect your identity.

Our colleague Lynette Hornung-Kobes wrote the following piece. She has worked for the Federal Department of Justice and also has private sector experience. It is a very thoughtful discussion of the balancing act that we must observe when legislating, regulating, and managing ID theft protection rules.

Identity Theft: Balancing the Need to Protect Privacy, Provide Security and Meet Business Need
By Lynette Hornung-Kobes

Identity theft is a complex problem for the government, private industry and consumers. The challenges are multifaceted and not easily solved. However, some positive steps have recently been taken by government largely led by the President's Identity Theft Task Force, which is headed by the Attorney General of the Department of Justice and the Federal Trade Commission Chairman. As government, private companies and consumers continue to try to combat identity theft, it will take creative problem solving to appropriately address the privacy and security needs, while simultaneously not making it impossible for government and private industry to conduct their business.

The Federal Identity Theft Task Force has focused on four areas: 1) securing consumer data, 2) preventing the misuse of consumer data, 3) victim recovery from identity theft, and 4) law enforcement efforts to prosecute and punish identity thieves (Federal Identity Theft Task Force).

Securing Consumer Data

To make consumers more secure, the Identity Theft Task Force has required federal agencies to review their collection and use of Social Security Numbers (SSNs). The Identity Theft Task Force has recommended that the Office of Management and Budget use a survey to evaluate how agencies protect sensitive consumer data that agencies maintain. It was also recommended that the Office of Personnel Management review the use of Social Security Numbers in human resources by federal agencies, and if it is not necessary to use the SSNs, then that practice should be eliminated. Since identity thieves often use the social security number of a person as an easy data type to commit identity theft, the Identity Theft Task Force is considering whether it should recommend that private industry evaluate and eliminate the unnecessary use of social security numbers (Federal Identity Theft Task Force). The Identity Theft Task Force is also considering whether a national breach notification should be required. Another topic under consideration is increased educational awareness for both private industry on protecting sensitive information and consumers on better safeguarding their personal data from identity theft.

Preventing the Misuse of Consumer Data

The Identity Theft Task Force is exploring solutions for providing more reliable ways of authenticating the identity of individuals, which would prevent identity thieves from gaining unlawful access and/or opening a new account with a stolen identity (Federal Identity Theft Task Force). To explore these types of solutions, the Task Force is considering holding a workshop or workshops with members of the academic community, members of industry and entrepreneurs. Academics, private industry professionals and entrepreneurs would all have a variety of knowledge, experience and understanding of various solutions that could provide more effective solutions for helping to protect and/or mitigate the misuse of consumer data.

Victim Recovery from Identity Theft

The Identity Theft Task Force is considering a variety of solutions to better assist victims of identity theft, which include providing training to law enforcement on how to better assist victims of identity theft, national training for identity theft assistance counselors, and exploring how to include other national service organizations in assisting victims of identity theft (Federal Identity Theft Task Force). Included in this area of focus is whether national laws need to be amended to better assist victims of identity theft in being able to recover from the damaging effects of identity theft. For example, does the ceiling need to be lowered in allowing a victim of identity theft to recover damages? Another consideration is an evaluation of state credit freeze laws to better understand what measures are more valuable to consumers.

Law Enforcement Efforts to Prosecute and Punish Identity Thieves

The Identity Theft Task Force is considering the recommendation of a National Identity Theft Law Enforcement

Center to facilitate the sharing of information among criminal and civil law enforcement agencies and if applicable, the private sector (Federal Identity Theft Task Force). Another consideration is for the Department of Justice to work more collaboratively on fraud prevention and increased public awareness of Section 609(e) of the Fair Credit Reporting Act with financial institutions and private industry. Section 609(e) allows identity theft victims to receive documents on this crime and to designate law enforcement agencies who can receive such documentation on their behalf (Federal Identity Theft Task Force). Identity theft is not just a domestic problem, it crosses national boundaries. The Department of Justice and Department of State can explore ways to work with other nations to combat identity theft. This may include re-evaluating electronic and other forms of evidence in criminal cases that may be used with law enforcement agencies in other nations. Federal statutes that pertain to identity theft may need revision to better address and provide legal remedy to victims of identity theft. For example, does 18 U.S.C. § 1030(a) that makes it a crime to steal electronic data sent through interstate communications, need to be amended to remove the interstate communication requirement? (Federal Identity Theft Task Force).

Clearly, Identity Theft is a complex problem. There are many entities that can work to assist consumers, from law enforcement agencies who investigate and prosecute such cases to banks and credit bureaus who can assist with credit freezes and other services to victims of identity theft. A good first step is to look at the frequently used common denominator, the Social Security Number, and how this important data type can be better protected. How can greater awareness of the appropriate protection against misuse of this and other sensitive data among government, private industry and by basic consumers be improved? Currently federal agencies are reviewing how they collect and maintain Social Security Numbers and, if this is not necessary, are exploring ways to eliminate it. Currently, whether private industry needs to do the same is also being explored. Also under consideration is whether data brokers need to be held more accountable in providing for protection of sensitive information that they may sell. As federal, state, and local government as well as private industry wrestle with how to protect and/or mitigate against data breaches, which feeds into the identity theft arena, there is the potential for a better approach to emerge. What is important is to balance the need to protect and/or mitigate against identity theft with the ability of government and industry to still be able to function, while working to provide adequate security to the privacy and/or sensitive information associated with a consumer's identity.

Currently, the federal government and private industry are dealing with how to deal with the loss of data from laptop theft, unencrypted data loss, theft or loss of backup tapes, hacker activity, insider threat, and other theft. The challenge for government and industry lies in how to protect against these threats that are part of identity theft without locking down and restricting the environment to the extent that neither government employees nor federal contractors can do their jobs. For example, if an agency comes up with a policy which requires all removable media to be encrypted, then what about a federal contractor's ability to provide client information on a CD when the encryption available is not robust enough to meet strong encryption standards? Also, what if the policy guidance in an agency comes up with a policy requirement, which prevents components in that agency from using technological tools to meet security requirements? How can components gain the needed flexibility to use their tools to meet security requirements when all of a sudden the rules have changed? It is critical that as federal agencies, state and local government and private industry all work to address some points of weakness with regard to identity theft, there is thoughtful consideration given to what strong policies seeking to make data more secure do not go so far into the realm of arbitrary enforcement that it makes it difficult, if not impossible for people to do their jobs, regardless of whether they are government employees or federal contractors. In other words, it is important not only to focus on the short-term solution, but also to think about the long-term consequences of such a policy and whether it is both a short term and long-term solution.

The President's Identity Theft Task Force has come up with a lot of good recommendations. One excellent starting point is for federal agencies to evaluate the use of Social Security Numbers and such use is not necessary, then their use should be eliminated. The Social Security Number is a frequently used data type to commit identity theft, so it should be adequately protected by government and private industry. Consumers need to be educated to understand how to better protect their Social Security Numbers from unnecessary use.

However, there are some basic data types that are important to protect to prevent identity theft. According to Stacy Collett, it is important to identify the appropriate data to protect (SSN, financial data, credit cards, health, and intellectual property) and then pursue effective strategies to protect this data, which include encryption and using technologies to protect data in transit on the back-end database. The challenge with encryption involves managing encryption keys and its effect on system performance. Identity Theft, as the Task Force recommended, is a complex problem, which will involve not only understanding sensitive data types to identify and protect, but also using technology to help meet the business or mission needs while providing for the security of privacy data and other sensitive data types. Hopefully federal agencies and private companies will work together to come up with quality solutions, which provide not only good short term, but also valuable long-term solutions.

Works Cited

Collett, Stacy. (2006). Encrypting Data at Rest: With a dizzying array of new encryption options on the market, which one is right for you? Computerworld. Retrieved from World Wide Web on 05/15/2007 from http://www.computerworld.com/hardwaretopics/storage/story/0,10801,109826,00.html

Federal Identity Theft Task Force. Retrieved from World Wide Web http://www.usdoj.gov/ittf/docs/issues_summary.pdf

See also President's Identity Theft Task Force: Summary of Interim Recommendations. Retrieved from World Wide Web http://www.usdoj.gov/ittf/docs/interimrecomm.pdf

Lynette Hornung-Kobes

Lynette is currently a Senior Computer Security and Privacy Consultant with Northrop Grumman Information Technology. She has supported a variety of Department of Justice components, including the Office of the Solicitor General and the Chief Security Officer in the DOJ Office of the Chief Information Officer with computer security and privacy support. She was an IT Security Specialist at the Department of Justice for two years prior to joining Northrop Grumman where she worked on Certification and Accreditation at the enterprise level for the Public Key Infrastructure, on the component level at United States National Central Bureau (Interpol) and at the application level for the System Development Services, including providing support to the Office of the Solicitor General.

Lynette is a NSF CyberCorps scholar and was a contributing author to a book on Identity Theft by Dr. Steffen Schmidt and Michael McCoy. Ms. Hornung-Kobes has been a speaker at NetSec, the Cyber Information Security Conference, and the Computer Security Institute on security and privacy topics. She was top speaker at the Cyber Information Security Conference, garnering higher evaluations than other seasoned computer security speakers.

One of the most interesting resolved cases is the Choice-Point data breach. We are providing you with information about its resolution because it promises to become a classic case study for business schools.

For Release: January 26, 2006
ChoicePoint Settles Data Security Breach Charges; to Pay $10 Million in Civil Penalties, $5 Million for Consumer Redress
At Least 800 Cases of Identity Theft Arose From Company's Data Breach

Consumer data broker ChoicePoint, Inc., which last year acknowledged that the personal financial records of more than 163,000 consumers in its database had been compromised, will pay $10 million in civil penalties and $5 million in consumer redress to settle Federal Trade Commission charges that its security and record-handling procedures violated consumers' privacy rights and federal laws. The settlement requires ChoicePoint to implement new procedures to ensure that it provides consumer reports only to legitimate businesses for lawful purposes, to establish and maintain a comprehensive information security program, and to obtain audits by an independent third-party security professional every other year until 2026.

"The message to ChoicePoint and others should be clear: Consumers' private data must be protected from thieves," said Deborah Platt Majoras, Chairman of the FTC. "Data security is critical to consumers, and protecting it is a priority for the FTC, as it should be to every business in America."

ChoicePoint is a publicly traded company based in suburban Atlanta. It obtains and sells to more than 50,000 businesses the personal information of consumers, including their names, Social Security numbers, birth dates, employment information, and credit histories.

The FTC alleges that ChoicePoint did not have reasonable procedures to screen prospective subscribers, and turned over consumers' sensitive personal information to subscribers whose applications raised obvious "red flags." Indeed, the FTC alleges that ChoicePoint approved as customers individuals who lied about their credentials and used commercial mail drops as business addresses. In addition, ChoicePoint applicants reportedly used fax machines at public commercial locations to send multiple applications for purportedly separate companies.

According to the FTC, ChoicePoint failed to tighten its application approval procedures or monitor subscribers even after receiving subpoenas from law enforcement authorities alerting it to fraudulent activity going back to 2001.

The FTC charged that ChoicePoint violated the Fair Credit Reporting Act (FCRA) by furnishing consumer reports – credit histories – to subscribers who did not have a permissible purpose to obtain them, and by failing to maintain reasonable procedures to verify both their identities and how they intended to use the information.

The agency also charged that ChoicePoint violated the FTC Act by making false and misleading statements about its privacy policies. Choicepoint had publicized privacy principles that address the confidentiality and security of personal information it collects and maintains with statements such as, "ChoicePoint allows access to your consumer reports only by those authorized under the FCRA . . . " and "Every ChoicePoint customer must successfully complete a rigorous credentialing process. ChoicePoint does not distribute information to the general public and monitors the use of its public record information to ensure appropriate use."

The stipulated final judgment and order requires Choice-Point to pay $10 million in civil penalties – the largest civil penalty in FTC history – and to provide $5 million for consumer redress. It bars the company from furnishing consumer reports to people who do not have a permissible purpose to receive them and requires the company to establish and maintain reasonable procedures to ensure that consumer reports are provided only to those with a permissible purpose. ChoicePoint is required to verify the identity of businesses that apply to receive consumer reports, including making site visits to certain business premises and auditing subscribers' use of consumer reports.

The order requires ChoicePoint to establish, implement, and maintain a comprehensive information security program designed to protect the security, confidentiality, and integrity of the personal information it collects from or about consumers. It also requires ChoicePoint to obtain, every two years for the next 20 years, an audit from a qualified, independent, third-party professional to ensure that its security program meets the standards of the order. ChoicePoint will be subject to standard record keeping and reporting provisions to allow the FTC to monitor compliance. Finally, the settlement bars future violations of the FCRA and the FTC Act.

This case is being brought with the invaluable assistance of the U.S. Department of Justice and the Securities and Exchange Commission.

The Commission vote to accept the settlement was 5-0.

Along with the fine levied against ChoicePoint in January, those actions suggest that the FTC views thwarting identity theft as a duty for businesses regardless of whether the provisions of Gramm-Leach-Bliley directly relate to them. Moreover, this action underscores the commission's authority under section 5 of the FTC Act to take action against companies that engage in lax security practices that could expose the personal financial information of customers to theft or loss.

NOTE: A stipulated final judgment and order is for settlement purposes only and does not constitute an admission by the defendant of a law violation. Consent judgments have the force of law when signed by the judge.

Copies of the complaint and stipulated final judgment and order are available from the FTC's Web site at http://www. ftc.gov and also from the FTC's Consumer Response Center, Room 130, 600 Pennsylvania Avenue, N.W., Washington, D.C. 20580. The FTC works for the consumer to prevent fraudulent, deceptive, and unfair business practices in the marketplace and to provide information to help consumer's spot, stop, and avoid them. To file a complaint in English or Spanish (bilingual counselors are available to take complaints), or to get free information on any of 150 consumer topics, call toll-free, 1-877-FTC-HELP (1-877-382-4357), or use the complaint form at http://www.ftc.gov. The FTC enters Internet, telemarketing, identity theft, and other fraud-related complaints into Consumer Sentinel, a secure, online database available to hundreds of civil and criminal law enforcement agencies in the U.S. and abroad.

Media Contact:
  Claudia Bourne Farrell,
  Office of Public Affairs
  202-326-2181

We have alluded to the Internet and given some examples of its risks in previous chapters. In Chapter 6 we will delve into this topic in greater detail. Even if you are not a computer geek, we feel that you need to understand the risks and some of the terminology that is commonly used.

CHAPTER 6
THE INTERNET AND IDENTITY THEFT

Internal Revenue Service (IRS) Warns Taxpayers of New E-mail Scams. Jan. 14, 2008 — A new variation of the refund scheme may be directed toward organizations that distribute funds to other organizations or individuals. In an attempt to seem legitimate, the scam e-mail claims to be sent by, and contains the name and supposed signature of, the Director of the IRS Exempt Organizations area of the IRS. The e-mail asks recipients to click on a link to access a form for a tax refund. In reality, taxpayers claim their tax refunds through the filing of an annual tax return, not a separate application form.

http://www.irs.gov/newsroom/article/0,,id=170894,00.html

The Internet is a wonderful thing but, as the IRS warning with which we opened this chapter suggests, it is also a place full of tricks and traps that can ensnare and hurt very badly the unsuspecting consumer.

Imagine that, unbeknownst to you, many people start coming into your house, putting audio bugs and surveillance cameras throughout your home. Then, like in Orwell's wonderful book 1984, the government as "Big Brother" knows everything you do and watches your every move. In the case of the Internet, it is "Big Secret Hacker" who can silently watch everything you are doing on your computer, copy and retrieve that information, and steal credit card, password and other information from you. They can even take over your computer without your knowledge and use it to route pornography and commit other crimes through your computer.

The Internet was created for military communications on a narrow and exclusive network (ARPANET) designed to continue operating even during war time. The World Wide Web was made "intelligent" so that any "lines or communication" cut by, say, a nuclear attack, would not disable the network. Instead it would automatically seek out ANY routes, no matter how unlikely, to send the packets of information to their final destination. This network consisted at first of individuals in the military and security sector. Most of them were certified to the extent that they had clearance and access to this military network. Therefore the issue of security or unauthorized access was minimal. They were all "authenticated" and cleared individuals.

This dedicated and secure network slowly started opening up to other users. At first it was universities especially academics and researchers, then students, and finally the general public. The "Net" rapidly expanded as personal computers came on the scene and replaced the expensive and huge "mainframe" units that required sophisticated programming knowledge and really complicated MS-DOS commands to operate.

This new open and public Internet was once seen as a place for nice people maximizing their individuality, connecting and communing with each other, and freeing everyone from commercialization by having most things for free. This fantasy world quickly degenerated into chaos as pornographers, hucksters, spammers, politicians, hate groups, and other undesirable people also settled into the world of cyberspace.

In order to be intelligent about the role of the Internet, you need to learn some terms that are commonly used in discussing the nasty side of cyberspace.

Adware - A form of spyware (see below) that collects information about the user in order to display advertisements in the Web browser based on the information it collects from the user's browsing patterns.

Hacking - Unauthorized use, or attempts to bypass the security mechanisms of an information system or network. Illegally breaking into a computer over the Internet or other networked access.

Keylogger/keylogging - A keylogger program is a piece of software that can be downloaded on purpose by someone who wants to monitor activity on a particular computer or it can be downloaded remotely as spyware and executed as part of a rootkit or remote administration (RAT) Trojan horse. It monitors each keystroke a person types on a specific computer's keyboard and that information (say you type in your credit card number) is then sent back to the person monitoring the information. http://searchsecurity.techtarget. com/sDefinition/0,,sid14_gci962518,00.html

Malware - Short for *mal*icious soft*ware*, such as a virus or a Trojan horse <u>software</u> designed specifically to damage or disrupt a system.

Rootkit – A standalone software component that attempts to hide processes, files, registry data, and network connections. They are often used for malicious purposes by viruses, worms, and "backdoors."

Spyware - Any software that covertly gathers user information through the user's Internet connection without his or her knowledge.

Spam/Spammer – Unwanted e-mail usually sent out in huge numbers like "junk mail."

Trojan Horse - A computer program in which harmful code is hidden inside apparently harmless programming or data in such a way that it can then quietly do bad things. There have been cases where programs that are supposed to find and destroy computer viruses are actually Trojan Horses that then distribute the viruses. The term comes from Greek mythology where a hollow horse sent as a gift was allowed into the fortified city and then at night the enemy soldiers hidden inside came out to wreak havoc. This is mentioned in Homer's Odyssey.

Virus – A program or piece of code that " … is loaded onto your computer without your knowledge and runs against your wishes. Viruses can also replicate themselves. All computer viruses are manmade. A simple virus that can make a copy of itself over and over again is relatively easy to produce. Even such a simple virus is dangerous because it will quickly use all available memory and bring the system to a halt. An even more dangerous type of virus is one capable of transmitting itself across networks and bypassing security systems." http://www.webopedia.com/TERM/V/virus.html

These terms identify some of the threats to your identity security. Now let's specifically identify other ways that your personal confidential information can be put at risk.

Phishing

You've probably heard about phishing, which is defined as *"... an attempt to **criminally** and **fraudulently** acquire sensitive information, such as usernames, **passwords** and credit card details, by masquerading as a trustworthy entity in an electronic communication. **eBay, PayPal** and **online banks** are common targets. Phishing is typically carried out by **email** or **instant messaging**,[1] and often directs users to enter details at a website, although phone contact has also been used. Phishing is an example of **social engineering** techniques used to fool users."*

http://en.wikipedia.org/wiki/Phishing

The reason this works so well for the criminals is the human motivation to answer an e-mail and willingly provide confidential information to something that appears reliable. That's why it is called a "social engineering" technique and is based on very sophisticated human behavioral responses. Most psychologists agree that this behavior is based largely on a person's trust instinct. Banks have traditionally been solid institutions, with big, steel safe, secure deposit boxes where you can lock up your valuable documents and jewelry, and where the solid, conservative "banker" will take good care of your financial assets. Therefore we have had no problem entrusting these people with our money and our valuables.

Another motivation for sharing sensitive information is what we call "branding trust." Here is a test - Think of the brand name you respect and admire (and trust) the most! What is it? Now, if you got something from them in your e-mail, you would be more likely to let your guard down because you respect this firm or organization (say, the Red Cross, or your church, or a trusted company).

Fortunately as we write this, most people have gotten more savvy to unsolicited e-mails asking for confidential information EVEN from trusted sources (e-Bay, or your bank) because we have been educated on the "Phishing Expeditions" that simulate these trusted sources. Most smart people do NOT answer or click on any email links from these phishing ID theft or financial theft criminals. But often it's hard to tell the bad guys from the trusted brands.

Now comes an advanced version of phishing called Spear Phishing because it's so precise and targeted at you (the fish!) when you are most vulnerable! According to Microsoft

Spear phishing describes any highly targeted phishing attack. Spear phishers send e-mail that appears genuine to all the employees or members within a certain company, government agency, organization, or group.

The message might look like it comes from your employer, or from a colleague who might send an e-mail message to everyone in the company, such as the head of human resources or the person who manages the computer systems, and could include requests for user names or passwords.

The truth is that the e-mail sender information has been

faked or "spoofed." Whereas traditional phishing scams are designed to steal information from individuals, spear phishing scams work to gain access to a company's entire computer system.

http://www.microsoft.com/protect/yourself/phishing/spear.mspx

These attacks against our security pose serious risks to personal identity information at two levels. First, at the personal computer level, consumers by the tens of thousands are tricked into opening their computers to security intrusions. Second, at the server or company, hospital, university or government level, this can result in a catastrophic breach with often millions of records compromised.

All of this has now become a fine art and a super sophisticated criminal enterprise. Consider the following story reported recently by PC World.

Wednesday, January 23, 2008. "Security researchers have discovered a group of hackers who are exploiting a new category of victims -- aspiring Internet scammers. A Moroccan group called "Mr. Brain" is offering free phishing kits on a Web site hosted in France, said Paul Mutton, Internet services developer at Netcraft, a security company in Bath, England. The software packages make it easy to quickly set up a fraudulent Web site mimicking a known brand in order to trick people into divulging credit card details or bank account numbers. Templates for spam e-mail are also included, targeting brands such as Bank of America, eBay, PayPal and HSBC.

Mr. Brain's Web site lists the kits and what kind of details each one is capable of collecting, such as usernames, pass-

words or Social Security numbers. Netcraft posted screen-shots on its Web site. But what the aspiring scammer doesn't know is that the phishing kits are designed to send any sen-sitive information that's collected back to e-mail accounts controlled by Mr. Brain.

Microsoft, 2008. http://www.pcworld.com/businesscen-ter/article/141688/scam_wars_phishing_kits_exploit_cus-tomers.html

This just proves the old adage that there is no honor among thieves!

Another instructive case is the attack several years ago against a port authority.

"… the head of security for a state port authority told of how a phisher - possibly a current or former employee, or someone in cahoots with one - bluffed his way onto the corporate network by first spoofing an internal e-mail address. The ploy, apparently designed to elicit application passwords, got responses from about 50 workers before one called the IT department to raise a red flag, according to a conference attendee."

"… the damage that can ensue is substantial, experts say. In the port authority case, the phisher could have found a number of ways into the corporate network once he con-vinced employees that his e-mail actually came from a co-worker. For example, the phisher could have attached a key-logging program to the e-mail that recorded an unsuspecting employee's password while he was accessing an application, thus granting the phisher access as well." (http://www.net-workworld.com/news/2005/013105phishing.html)

This is clearly a disturbing example of how phishing can break into systems. A port authority has a huge database of records of employees, of ship captains and crew, of security personnel and, of course, has security codes used to protect port facilities. The risks of any of this data being accessed by unauthorized people, raises both risks for individual identity theft but also poses huge risks for terrorist attacks.

One problem is that it's easy to say "be careful and never give information to anyone asking you to do anything." But what if you get an e-mail from your supervisor and she/he asks you to update your account and passwords because there has been some "suspicious" activity on the net at your organization/department? How often do you ignore such requests? In our organization we all suddenly got an email from one of our senior colleagues. It had his correct return email address. When we clicked, it opened up some pretty nasty pornography. Someone had hacked his email list, simulated his email, and maybe even taken control of his email system on his own computer, and sent this embarrassing porn to all of his contacts.

Another example where sensitive information was heisted from dropping illegal software on a bank computer (possibly through spear phishing or a simple "traditional" hack) comes from England.

A keystroke-logging system that allegedly allowed hackers to steal computer passwords is thought to be at the heart of a failed attempt to steal £229 million ($437m) from the London branch of a Japanese bank.

The attempted cyber-heist at the Sumitomo Mitsui Bank was first detected by the bank in October 2004, and the police were informed. But it only become public on Thursday after a man was arrested in Israel for allegedly preparing a bank account to receive nearly £14 million ($27m) of the bank's cash. (http://www.newscientist.com/channel/info-tech/electronic-threats/dn7168)

It is impossible and impractical to ask individuals to be pervasively aware and defensive about spear fishing in particular because essentially it would mean that you'd NEVER take any action or follow any instructions coming, in this case from your own company, university, church, blog group, college, or other organization(s) to which you belong! That, it seems to us would render e-mail virtually useless!

Imagine an e-mail from the Director of your working group – "Here are some of the new designs for our marketing initiative. Please let me know what you think and rank them 1, 2, 3".

Do you click or not? Do you make a phone call or try a face-to-face with the director – "Did YOU send out that e-mail?"

Clearly spear phishing poses a huge risk to the utility of e-mail as a tool for communication and interaction.

Microsoft has a major anti-phishing initiative and they recommend that consumers follow these practices to minimize the risks of being victimized by phishing:

• Never reveal personal or financial information in a response to an e-mail request, no matter who appears to have sent it.

• If you receive an e-mail message that appears suspicious, call the person or organization listed in the "From" line before you respond or open any attached files.

• Never click links in an e-mail message that requests personal or financial information. Enter the Web address into your browser window instead.

• Report any e-mail that you suspect might be a spear phishing campaign within your company.

• Use Internet Explorer 7 or the Windows Live Toolbar, both of which contain Phishing Filter, which scans and helps identify suspicious Web sites, and provides up-to-the-hour updates and reporting on known phishing sites.

In response to the serious risk of phishing and spear phishing, specific companies and industry groups have sprung up to address this issue. The three most prominent are:

• The Anti-Phishing Working Group
• Digital Phishnet
• Trusted Electronic Communications Forum

The Anti-Phishing Working Group is a terrifically interesting source of information on fishing and is worth a visit at http://www.antiphishing.org/

The Anti-Phishing Working Group (APWG) is the global pan-industrial and law enforcement association focused on eliminating the fraud and identity theft that result from phishing, pharming and email spoofing of all types.

This organization has over 3000 members, 1700+ companies & agencies worldwide, 9 of the top 10 US banks, and the top 5 US Internet Service Providers. The group reported a substantial spike in phishing at the end of 2007 amounting to a 28% increase over the previous high.

There is also a super cool animation that shows in real time phishing attacks and where they come from. On the day we are writing this, it is German attacks that are depicted by InternetPerils, which is the site that facilitates this. You can also check out a map of the world called the Crimeware Map. Here you can check by types of cyber attacks and see on the map where the attacks originate (see map below)

The Publishing and Crimeware map displays the most recent data collected by Websense Security Labs (WS Labs) and provides a historical look into where Phishing and Crimeware related websites are hosted on the internet. Upon discivery, each site is looked up via its IP Address to track the country of origin through the appropriate IP registrars and plotted on the map. The data is updated approximately 15 minutes after discovery.

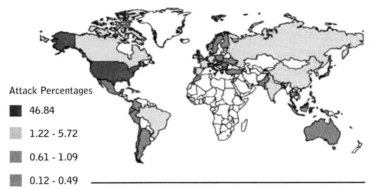

Attack Percentages

46.84

1.22 - 5.72

0.61 - 1.09

0.12 - 0.49

These organizations carry out a series of functions including information sharing, devising technical solutions, working with law enforcement agencies, improving information flow between industry and law enforcement to catch phishers, devising and promoting technology standards for the industry, as well as educating consumers, law enforcement personnel, government leaders, and the media.

FYI: In November 2004, British firm MessageLabs scanned over 80 million emails per day on behalf of its clients "We scanned more than 1.75 billion emails worldwide for spam, of which over 1.29 billion or 73.77% (1 in 1.36) were stopped as spam (498 per second).During the same period, we also scanned 2.11 billion emails for viruses, Trojans and other malicious content. More than 62.91 million or 2.98% (or 1 in 33.54) were intercepted (24 per second)."

Now that we've looked at this mode of operations let's review another malicious form of identity and security theft.

Pharming

The three "P's" of computing are - Phishing, Spear Phishing and Pharming. These cute terms define a series of variants on a theme which at its core is simple. Fool people into giving away valuable personal or company information and if necessary steal people's identities. Wikipedia, a user transforming encyclopedia, defines Pharming this way:

__Pharming__ is the _exploitation_ of a _vulnerability_ in the _DNS server software_ that allows a hacker to acquire the _Domain Name_ for a site, and to redirect traffic from that website to another web site. DNS servers are the _machines_ responsible for resolving internet names into their real _addresses_ - the "signposts" of the _internet_. If the web site receiving the traffic is a fake web site, such as a copy of a _bank's_ website, it can be used to _"phish"_ or steal a computer user's _passwords, PIN number_ or _account_ number.

(http://en.wikipedia.org/wiki/Pharming)

The technique, in case you are still not clear on how it works, is different from phishing where you get an e-mail saying your e-bay account security needs to be upgraded and send us your username and password.

Let's see if we can get some more detail on how nefarious

this process might be by looking at a good post by Edward W. Felten at Freedom to Tinker (http://www.freedom-to-tinker.com/?p=781).

"Pharming" attacks the translation process, to trick your computer somehow into accepting a false translation. If your computer accepts a false translation for "citibank.com," then when you communicate with "citibank.com" your packets will go to the villain's IP address, and not to the IP address of Citibank. ... here's the scary part: if a pharming attack is successful, there is no information on your computer to indicate that anything is wrong. As far as your computer (and the software on it) is concerned, everything is working fine, and you really are talking to "citibank.com." Worse yet, the attack can redirect all of your Citibank-bound traffic — email, online banking, and so on — to the villain's computer.

This is clearly a serious threat to personal as well as company security. We have wondered for many years how the geniuses in Silicon Valley, at MIT, the other leading tech schools, and in Redmond, Washington manage to miss the possibility of pharming happening. It's always amazing to us that this industry grew huge without spending very much time at all on the serious and dangerous issues of security.

The distressing and disconcerting thing about all of this is that we've reached the point where the consumer and Internet user has no idea what constitutes a dangerous site where evil is lurking and what's a benign or even helpful site. For example, on the homepage of pharming.org we find that there are pharming conscious and non-conscious (Non-PHC) web sites. See the following table:

We recommend that you DO NOT use the following sites, as they MAY NOT be pharming conscious (PhC) based on the last time we checked:

BANKING

bankofamerica.com • bankone.com
chase.com • cbbank.com • firstfedic.com
golden1creditunion.com • lasallebank.com
nationalcity.com • navyfcu.org • scefcu.org
tdwaterhouse.com • usbank.com • wachova.com
wamu.com • zionbank.com

BROKERAGE

sharebuilder.com

E-COMMERCE

bidnip.com

E-MAIL

msn.com • yahoo.com

TRAVEL

aa.com • continental.com • united.com

OTHER

blockbuster.com • gomillion.net • slashdot.org

CREDIT CARD

discovercard.com • mbna.com • providian.com

So WHAT exactly is it that we are not supposed to click on!?

Do we have the time to analyze every web page, scrutinize it for potential pharming risks (and we still don't get what it is we are looking for!), before clicking? Are we to go to pharming and phishing warning sites and see if a site we are about to visit is safe or not? If that's the case, we are doomed to never clicking on any links since they all look different and many, frankly look suspicious from the git go especially car rental and hotel web sites!

The "pharming" web site seems to be big on using only – may we call it "pharm-fresh!" sites. This is the advice :

Only use pharming-conscious or (PC) web sites. A PC web site uses a secure connection to prevent other web sites from impersonating it. PC web sites typically use the HTTPS web protocol on their login page to allow the user to verify the web site's identity. If an attacker attempts to impersonate a PC web site, the user will receive a message from the browser indicating that the web site's "certificate" does not match the address being visited. (Click here to see what an example of this message looks like. Users should **NEVER** click Yes in response to such a window, otherwise they might get duped by a pharming attack.)

But, frankly we did not click on any of the suggested hot links (like "click here" above - yeah right!) because we are so worried that this **whole site** is a pharming front! We just wanted out of there as fast as we could skedaddle!

By the way, here are some of the sites recommended at the time this piece was written – the web site suggests that "…you use the following sites, as they are pharming conscious (PC) based on the last time we checked:" This list early in 2008 is obviously incomplete and only applies to major companies.

Our "product loyalty" criterion for "trusting" well-known, and high quality services or products works for these well known sites. However, what are we supposed to do about sites that are not on this list since we travel on airlines other than Southwest, have email that may not be gmail, and so forth.

In reality we as consumers are, to a large extent, really standing fairly alone and vulnerable. There is no way that a single computer owner and user can be knowledgeable about all these web sites and their risks or threats. In most cases people and organizations don't even know what the risk is!

Finally, we think you should know about Zombie computers.

Zombie Computers

The most recent report on zombie computers we found is a truly chilling story that takes on science fiction quality. The Wired Magazine web site reported the following early in 2008

"Every security geek's favorite zombie computer army from 2007 -- the Storm Worm botnet -- has a new trick for 2008, using its huge collection of infected computers to send out phishing emails directing people to fake banking sites that it cleverly also hosts on the computers it remotely controls. The new campaign may indicate, according to F-Secure, that Storm's controllers have figured out how to divide the massive army into clusters which it is now renting out to others.

The Storm Worm botnet got its start last January [2007] with a spam email purporting to have information about the storms that were battering Europe at the time. Users with unpatched Windows machines who clicked on the link in the email were infected with a Trojan that joined the machine to the zombie army.

Storm's controllers use peer-to-peer communication to tell individual machines what to do -- making it impossible to decapitate the army by finding and shutting down the central server that the infected PCs call home to. Storm also seemed to have a mechanism to fight back at security researchers who probed infected computers. Security experts found that their research efforts could lead Storm to direct a torrent of traffic back at them if they weren't careful about disguising where they were coming from.

http://blog.wired.com/27bstroke6/2008/01/zombie-computer.html

We don't know about you, but this is starting to look like the bad guys are more powerful, more impertinent, and more agile than the good guys. The hijacking of computers and using them as "living dead" computers to commit crimes is no joke. We have always been surprised that rather than relegating this to the world of computer researchers, this has not become priority number one for governments such as the US and Canada. Clearly these zombie computers are a threat to individual identity information. However, they are also a clear and real danger to the national security of states.

In a piece entitled "Call to quarantine zombie computers: ISPs must do more to stop zombie attacks," Dinah Greek, of Computeract!ve writes on the VNU Network, on June 2, 2005 that:

"Consumers could find their internet connections taken down or severely curtailed if Internet service providers (ISPs) follow new guidelines. An international governmental anti-spam consortium, the London Action Plan (LAP) has called on ISPs to tackle the growing problem of zombie networks and quarantine customers whose PCs have been hijacked to send spam and viruses."

In a very interesting piece "An Army of Soulless 1's and 0's", Stephen Labaton of the New York Times wrote;

"Experts say hundreds of thousands of computers each

week are being added to ranks of zombies--commandeered computers--infected with software that makes them suscep-tible to remote deployment for a variety of illicit purposes, from overwhelming Web sites with traffic to cracking com-plicated security codes; user of zombie computer in most instances is never aware that it has been commandeered; networks of zombie computers are used for a variety of pur-poses, from attacking Web sites of companies and govern-ment agencies to generating huge batches of spam e-mail; officials at FBI and Justice Department say their inquiries on zombie networks are exposing serious vulnerabilities in Internet that could be exploited more widely by saboteurs to bring down Web sites or online messaging systems ..."

According to experts, the European Union leads the world in the number of zombie computers. Around the world in 2005, an average of 172,000 new PCs were infected each month.

Ms. Greek writes in her VNU Network article:

These networks are typically controlled by hackers oper-ations, such as spamming and [JB] denial of service attacks. However, increasingly they are being used for other illegal activities such as storing child abuse images and phishing sites. By routing emails through zombie computers or using these PCs to host websites with illegal activities, spammers or hackers are able to hide the origin of junk mail and make it more difficult for law enforcement agencies to find them. Because zombie networks are such a serious threat, Richard Cox of anti spam organisation, Spamhaus said the only way to tackle the issue at the moment was to take affected cus-tomers offline.

The BBC also reported that although we have known about, detected, and when possible cleaned up, we have not know the scale of "zombification" taking place:

Data was gathered using machines that looked innocent but which logged everything hackers did to them. The detailed look at zombie or 'bot nets of hijacked computers was done by the [German component of] Honeynet Project - a group of security researchers that gather information using networks of computers that act as "honey pots" to attract hackers and gather information about how they work.

What the surveillance team did was to create software that logs what happens to sacrificial, easy to hack computers that the group put out on the World Wide Web as sacrificial PC's. The conclusions of the group were that:

Getting the machines hijacked was worryingly easy. The longest time a Honeynet machine survived without being found by an automatic attack tool was only a few minutes. The shortest compromise time was only a few seconds.

Why should the average "civilian" be interested in, much less concerned about, zombies? Again the BBC report is very instructive:

During the monitoring period, the team saw 'bot nets used to launch 226 distributed denial-of-service attacks on 99 separate targets. These attacks bombard websites with data in an attempt to overwhelm the target. Other 'bot nets were used to abuse the Google Adsense program that rewards websites for displaying advertisements from the search engine.

Some zombie networks were used to attack and manipulate online polls and games. The abuse in this area raises frightening problems for things such as Internet voting which has been discussed and which is being actively experimented with in several states.

The final conclusion of the BBC report is most pertinent to our concerns when it said that

Criminals also seem to be starting to use 'bot nets for mass identity theft, to host websites that look like those of banks so confidential information can be gathered and to peep into online traffic to steal sensitive data.

Internet Service Providers can usually tell a computer may be a zombie. Isolating these units in a "walled garden" (i.e. not letting them go out to the Internet), notifying the customer, and helping them clean their computers is the major recommended way of dealing with this huge problem.

However, this security activity will cost ISP's millions upon millions of dollars and many are not likely to want to incur that cost. Moreover, weary computer owners and users will surely be nervous about and reluctant to follow the ISP orders since nowadays they fear any messages coming in their e-mail that say the mail is from some entity (in this case the ISP), especially a message that may ask them to download something to help with the fix!

Another very interesting development is the long-term consequences of computer contamination. Contamination is now widespread. The **Pew Group** recently reported that 43 percent of the 2,001 adult Internet users polled said they had been affected by spyware or adware. Forty-eight percent said they no longer surfed Web sites that they felt would place unwanted programs on their computers. A whopping 68% percent reported that they had had computer problems in the last year that looked like the problems that were caused by spyware or adware.

"The threat of spyware and other unwanted software programs is changing the way people use the Internet, according to a survey of US net users from the Pew Internet and American Life Project.

Nine out of ten Internet users quizzed said they'd "adjusted their online behavior" out of fear of falling victim to malware attacks. Pew notes that user fears are often grounded in personal experience. A quarter (25 per cent) of net users have spotted new programs or desktop icons on their PCs that they hadn't installed. One in five Internet users (18 per cent) have had their homepage inexplicably changed. Both are common signs of malware infection."

http://www.theregister.com/2005/07/07/spyware_survey_pew/

The Pew survey also found the following:

- 81% of net users say they have stopped opening unsolicited email attachments
- 48% say they have stopped visiting certain web sites out of fear of getting spyware
- 25% of those questioned said they have stopped downloading music or video files from peer-to-peer networks to avoid getting contaminated
- 18% say they have changed the web browser software they use in order to avoid malware attacks.

Computer savvy experts (gearheads) are now suggesting that if a computer is severely contaminated with malware – spyware, viruses, adware – it's cheaper and easier to throw the computer away and buy a $400-$500 replacement. In our own conversations with computer experts, we found this confirmed; many even suggested that once a computer is contaminated, it may actually be impossible to clean the hard drive of all the malicious programs. (New York Times, July 17, 2005).

So in the face of all this, what is a consumer, company, or organization to do?

Obviously there should be good security software in place and ISP's and company or government server managers need to have robust firewalls and security procedures in place. Still for the individual consumer our advice early in 2008 remains the same throughout this book. Hire some security help in making sure that the pharmers, phishers, hackers, and other miscreants don't wreck your life. The best help is some form of proven identity theft protection and insurance. We will remind the reader repeatedly in this book of the wisdom of such protection and we have rated some of the services available and discussed this in more detail in other parts of the book.

We found the following column by Dr. Kabay to be very interesting since it puts a human and specific face on who is involved in systematic Id theft.

Identity Theft (2): The Shadowcrew Case
by M. E. Kabay, PhD, CISSP-ISSMP
CTO, School of Graduate Studies
Norwich University, Northfield VT

In my last column in this series on identity theft, I introduced some statistical resources about the problem. Today I'll begin discussing some of the nasty techniques used for identity theft and how to defend oneself against them.

Stealing physical credit cards and creating fake ones are

part of the criminal technique called "carding." One of the significant recent successful investigations and prosecutions of an international credit-card fraud ring began with the US Secret Services's Operation Firewall in late 2004. The investigators discovered a network of over 4,000 members communicating through the Internet and conspiring to use phishing, spamming, forged identity documents (e.g., fake driver's licenses), creation of fake plastic credit cards, resale of gift cards bought with fake credit cards, fencing of stolen goods via eBay, and interstate or international funds transfers using electronic money such as E-Gold and Web Money.

In October 2004, the Department of Justice (DOJ) indicted 19 of the leaders of Shadowcrew; http://www.usdoj.gov/criminal/cybercrime/mantovaniIndict.htm By November 2005, 12 of these people had already pleaded guilty to charges of conspiracy and trafficking in stolen credit card numbers with losses of more than $4M. http://www.usdoj.gov/criminal/cybercrime/mantovaniPlea.htm

In February 2006, Shadowcrew leader Kenneth J. Flury, 41, of Cleveland, OH was sentenced to 32 months in prison with 3 years of supervised release and $300K in restitution to Citibank. http://www.usdoj.gov/criminal/cybercrime/flurySent.htm In June 2006, co-founder Andrew Mantovani, 24, of Scottsdale AZ was fined $5K and also received 32 months of prison with 3 years of supervised release. Five other indicted Shadowcrew criminals were sentenced with him. By that time, a total of 18 of 28 indicted suspects had already pleaded guilty. http://www.usdoj.gov/usao/nj/press/files/mant0629_r.htm

One of the lessons we teach our "CJ341 Cyberlaw & Cybercrime" students at Norwich University is that everyone with a credit card ought to check his/her statement immediately upon receiving it. Every line should be recognizable; if it is not, call your credit-card company to find out what a particular charge is for and where it was charged. Tell your company to freeze your card account if there is any question of its having been compromised. Write down the details of every conversation with the credit-card company employees (date, time, name of employee, case number) in case you need evidence to clear your own name. Contact the three major credit-reporting agencies (Equifax http://www.equifax.com/ , Experian < http://www.experian.com/ , and TransUnion http://www.transunion.com/) to tell them to freeze your credit report to make it harder for criminals to apply for loans or open bank accounts in your name until you release your credit records when you want to, not when the criminals want to.

Another tool is to ask for your free annual credit report on yourself from each of the three credit-reporting agencies using the official AnnualCreditReport site. https://www.annualcreditreport.com > You may want to ask for one report every four months by spacing out your requests to the three agencies so that you can spot unexpected changes (e.g., a request for a car loan in a state 3,000 miles from your home) more quickly than if you order all three at once. The AnnualCreditReport.com site mentioned above also provides extensive information in its Frequently Asked Questions <https://www.annualcreditreport.com/cra/helpfaq that will help consumers interact effectively with the agencies.

I hope that you will find this information useful for yourselves and for your colleagues and employees. I remind readers that I own the copyright to all my Network World articles and that my colleagues at Network World and I are delighted if you choose to use them verbatim in your internal security newsletters. There is no charge and you do not have to ask us for permission. However, if you do use these articles, please have the courtesy to include a pointer to the URL of the article in the Network World Security Strategies archive.

* * *

M. E. Kabay, PhD, CISSP-ISSMP is Program Director of the Master of Science in Information Assurance   http://www.graduate.norwich.edu/infoassurance/   and CTO of the School of Graduate Studies at Norwich University in Northfield, VT. Web site at   http://www2.norwich.edu/mkabay/index.htm .

Copyright © 2008 M. E. Kabay. All rights reserved.

Since we have many colleagues and associates in Canada or who work back and forth across the border, we wanted to share some interesting information about ID theft issues in Canada. Chapter 7 reviews some very interesting problems as well as Canadian legal solutions.

CHAPTER 7
IDENTITY THEFT IN CANADA

"Ontario Becomes First Canadian Jurisdiction With Credit Alert Legislation QUEEN'S PARK, Jan. 23, 2008 - In an ongoing effort to combat identity theft in Ontario, the McGuinty government has given consumers the ability to place an alert on their personal credit file, Government and Consumer Services Minister Ted McMeekin said today. Identity theft includes the use of someone else's personal information, without his or her knowledge or consent, to commit a crime such as fraud, theft or forgery. As of January 1, 2008, Ontario's new credit alert requirements ensure that lenders who receive information from a consumer's file will be told if there is an alert in place. Once informed of the alert, they must take action to verify the identity of the person before proceeding with transactions."

2008, http://www.newswire.ca/en/releases/archive/January2008/23/c3473.html

Identity theft is an international problem. As nations become more interdependent and as data sharing grows, the problems of preventing ID theft are no longer confined only to a national level, much less state, provincial, or local levels. It is curious but understandable that reporting ID theft is still largely left up to victims who must report to their LOCAL police department and initiate a complaint. However, as the inevitable truth sinks in that ID theft is a growing epidemic, actions such as those noted above in Ontario, Canada and in the U.S. that allow consumers to freeze their credit ratings in order to prevent unauthorized use of this root information, which leads to so much crime, are becoming more common-place

Voice of America (VOA) News reported that Identity theft has become a worldwide crime and cost consumers in Britain, Australia, and Canada $6 Billion (U.S.) according to the last report compiled. In Japan, thieves stole the financial records of 4.5 million subscribers to an Internet service provider. The South African publication Personal Finance reported on January 26, 2008 that a new law to curtail identity fraud seeks to protect South Africans from "… fraudsters who want access to your personal details, including the treasure trove of information often found on pay slips. A piece by Neesa Moodley-Isaacs explains

"Your employer will have to be more circumspect with the amount of personal information it prints on your pay slip when the Protection of Personal Information Bill comes into force later this year. Clayton Thomopoulos, the head of fraud prevention at Liberty Life Group Forensic Services, says employers in the public and private sectors are unwittingly facilitating identity theft by providing detailed personal and

financial information on pay slips. ...stolen identity numbers are used on marriage certificates to secure South African citizenship for illegal immigrants."

http://www.persfin.co.za/index.php?fArticleId=4224618&fSectionId=592&fSetId=300

As reported by the Ontario Ministry of Government and Consumer Affairs, a March 2006 Ipsos Reid study found that 25% of Canadian adults have either been victims of identity theft or know someone who has been a victim. A Fall 2005 study conducted by Ipsos-Reid found that 77% of Canadians were concerned about becoming victims of identity theft in the future. PhoneBusters reported that in 2006, over three thousand? 3,353 Ontarians were victims of identity theft and experienced losses of $7.6 million (U.S.).

Identity theft happens all over the world. We are working on a new book on identity theft in many different countries and the convoluted almost incomprehensible difficulties in stopping identity theft or arresting ID thieves in countries around the world. Although Interpol (the international police) and many bilateral law enforcement efforts are underway to enforce identity protection, the laws of sovereign countries and the internal workings of governments across the 200+ nations makes it a very complex picture indeed.

For example there was a case recently of a call center employee in India who allegedly sold personal data on 1,000 British customers. India has since announced that it will tighten laws to prevent cyber crimes and ensure data secrecy. The British government called Interpol to help with this case. However, as more and more business is handled by call centers around the world (including many in the Caribbean, Guyana, Belize, Africa, and other English speaking countries), the likelihood of similar incidents is very high.

Have you called a credit card company or an airline recently to get customer service? Did you guess that the person to whom you were speaking was in Pakistan, India, or some other country outside the legal jurisdiction of the United States or Canada? Did you even for a moment think about how easy it would be for all that sensitive information about you to be passed on to others and how hard it would be for you to file a charge, get an investigation going, have an arrest warrant issued thousands of miles away, and present yourself in court there if an arrest were made?

Our colleagues in Europe and Canada and we have now started discussing the need for an international identity theft and loss treaty and convention. We also believe that new and more robust identity theft services, which includes international legal counsel with certified attorneys in countries with high critical information theft, is necessary.

We offer this chapter on ID theft in Canada because we have been doing some work with colleagues there in ID theft protection and prevention. Moreover, financial credit reporting services in the United States and Canada cooperate with each other and overlap and therefore ID theft protection, prevention, and recovery are somewhat similar. In Canada the personal ID number at greatest risk, similar to the American Social Security number is called the Social Insurance Number (SIN).

In 2003, the Canada-United States Cross-Border Crime Forum determined that a threat assessment on identity theft and its impact on criminal behavior across the border of the two countries were necessary. A Cross-Border Mass Marketing Fraud working group was established in order to pinpoint and then recommend action related to these types of crimes.

The initial report from the working group very clearly spells out why ID theft is such a huge threat.

... identity theft is committed in every place associated with daily life. Identity thieves target residences, workplaces and even places of recreation. Moreover, the growing ubiquity of digital data, and of computers and devices that transmit or store such data, means that identity thieves can ply their trade without ever coming into physical proximity with the individuals whose data they are stealing.

Simply by doing things that are part of everyday routines -- for example, charging dinner at a restaurant, using payment cards to purchase gasoline or rent a car, or submitting personal information to employers and various levels of government -- individuals may be leaving or exposing their personal data where identity thieves can access and use it without the victim's knowledge or permission. The victim may not discover the effects of the fraud until weeks, months or even years later.

Source: http://www.publicsafety.gc.ca/prg/le/bs/report-en.asp; See also the Privacy Commission of Canada at http://www.privcom.gc.ca/fs-fi/02_05_d_10_e.asp

We highly commend the working group for making clear that ID theft often cannot be discovered for years after a data loss takes place. We also want to underscore the absolute irresponsibility of entities and organizations that lose or have data hacked who in their press release after discovering a break will almost always say, "We have no evidence that this sensitive information has been used for criminal behavior." Two weeks or two months after massive data loss of course there is not yet any evidence of criminal use. That's because smart crooks take their time, look over the information they have, sell it on the Internet to other crooks (yes, there are web sites where identity thieves sell Social Security numbers, drivers' license, credit card and other information), and commit the crimes much later, usually after the six month or one year free "credit report monitoring" that is given by organizations to the victims of their data loss is over.

The Public Safety Canada report also identifies who the most common ID thieves are and they identify the following three categories:

Comprehensive statistics on the perpetrators of identity theft are lacking and available data on identity thieves is largely anecdotal. However, this data indicates that identity thieves tend to fall into three broad categories:

* Members of organized criminal groups or networks

Law enforcement agencies in both countries are aware that organized crime groups such as outlaw motorcycle gangs and various ethnically based criminal organizations, as well as more locally based criminal networks, are increasingly involved in identity theft. These groups use identity theft not only to systematically make money but also to use the proceeds to support other criminal ventures. In addition, they may create a ready pool of others' identities to facilitate the commission of criminal activity and avoid detection by law enforcement.

* Terrorists

Governments in both countries are aware that terrorists

use identity theft to obtain cover employment, finance their activities and avoid detection when carrying out their attacks. For example, an al-Qaida terrorist cell in Spain used stolen credit cards in fictitious sales scams and for numerous other purchases. They kept purchases below amounts where identification would need to be presented. They also used stolen telephone and credit cards for communications back to Pakistan, Afghanistan, Lebanon, etc. Extensive use of false passports and travel documents were used to open bank accounts where money for the mujahideen movement was sent between countries such as Pakistan, Afghanistan, etc.

* Individual criminals

Identity theft is not committed only by organized groups or networks. Many individuals have used identity theft as a means to make money quickly, to obtain a benefit to which they are not otherwise entitled and to misdirect law enforcement away from the real perpetrators of crimes.

Source: http://www.publicsafety.gc.ca/prg/le/bs/report-en.asp

The Canadian report also has some excellent and very detailed examples of concrete cases of identity theft in Canada. The following is a good example of how this happens and also how to therefore develop defensive strategies.

Example -- Identities stolen from company database

A temporary replacement worker assigned to the office of a national financial services company in Ontario stole customer profiles from the company database. The company had thousands of profiles in the database and was unaware that the thefts had taken place. Numerous medical doctors began finding themselves the victims of identity theft in the form of false applications for credit being attributed to their name. The profiles that were stolen contained complete financial data on the doctors and their families.

The fraud source came to light when an officer stopped a vehicle as part of a routine operation and found the passenger in possession of several profiles. The officer was unable to effect an arrest as no offence was being committed at the time. He was unaware that the profiles were stolen and no credit card data existed on the profile sheets. The officer had the presence of mind to have the documents photocopied and turned over to fraud investigators.

An investigation identified the source of the compromise and an acknowledgement from the company that they were the source resulted in charges against the employee. Over one million dollars in fraud was attributed to the data theft and the incident resulted in charges against four individuals, to date, including the occupants of the car originally stopped. This case had over 100 victims from across Canada and resulted in frauds being perpetrated across the country. Obtaining a complete list of victims was problematic because of the lack of correlation of victims' names between the credit grantors, the credit bureaus, the police, the victims and the source company.

Source: http://www.publicsafety.gc.ca/prg/le/bs/report-en.asp

The United States and Canada have cooperated closely in the area of regulation and law enforcement to address the terrible spreading problem of identity theft. The following is a short and not completely up-to-date inventory of how Canada has been strengthening the law enforcement and regulatory environment.

Compilation and Analysis of Identity Theft Complaints

The Identity Theft and Assumption Deterrence Act vested the United States Federal Trade Commission with authority to establish a database of complaints from the public about identity theft. The database, now known as the Identity Theft Data Clearinghouse, is accessible by U.S. and Canadian law enforcement authorities that sign confidentiality agreements with the FTC.

Canadian Criminal Code

While in Canada there is no generalized offence called identity theft, there are a number of offences in the Criminal Code that criminalize activities integral to the criminal misuse of personal information. For example, subsection 342(3) of the Criminal Code criminalizes the possession, use of or trafficking in credit card and debit card data in such a way that would allow the perpetrator to use either the credit card or debit card itself or to obtain the services provided by the issuer of the card. The forgery provisions apply to persons who make false documents, with knowledge that the documents are false, and with intent that they should be used or acted on as genuine. A person who actually uses a false document, knowing that the document is forged, to defraud another person can be charged with fraud and with uttering a forged document. Perpetrators who assume a false identity in order to gain an economic or other advantage (such as to avoid detection for criminal offences) can be charged with impersonation. These provisions are illustrative of a number of the current provisions in the Criminal Code that address various aspects of identity theft.

Sources: Canadian Bankers Association, "Identity Theft:

An Old Problem Needing a New Approach"; "PhoneBusters Identity Theft Statistics", RCMP-CCB Ottawa; http://www. publicsafety.gc.ca/prg/le/bs/report-en.asp#_ftn19

In response to identity theft the Canadian government has swung into action and it has done so aggressively, with a great deal of transparency, coordination, and focus. In addition to tougher laws as described above, Canada has developed several fast and very impressive remediation and help services.

One excellent ID theft information source for Canada is Safecanana, which can be accessed on the Internet at http://www.safecanada.ca/identitytheft_e.asp. This web site, sponsored by the government of Canada is an excellent source of information on all aspects of ID theft. It is interesting and very useful even if you don't live in Canada and we highly recommend that you visit the site.

The Royal Canadian Mounted police (RCMP) have compiled some information on certain aspects of Canadian identity theft, which is available on line at http://www.phonebusters.com/english/statistics.html

Have you ever gotten one of those Nigerian Scam letters asking you to help unlock millions of dollars from a deceased Nigerian and in exchange you get millions for helping? Ever wonder if anyone actually falls for that trick? The RCMP reported almost 4 million dollars in losses!

Apparently Canadians, for some reason, fall for this scam more than Americans or Brits with 199 Canadian victims in 2004, 175 in 2005, and 190 in 2006. They also reported over $96 million dollars in losses from all kinds of scams and schemes (many of them related to fraudulent vacation and travel offers) in 2006.

Public Safety Canada reports that phishing has become a major Internet scam, which can lead to identity theft loss.

"The term phishing refers to luring techniques used by identity thieves to fish for personal information in a pond of unsuspecting Internet users".

Canada's Department of Public Safety and Emergency Preparedness and the United States Department of Justice are jointly issuing this special report to advise the public about the risks of responding to phishing emails and websites, and the steps to take when they encounter them."

Canada has also established a coordinated reporting center for fraud and ID theft. We are providing the following detailed information on what to do if you have a Canada related data or ID theft incident because you don't want to have to go searching for it at that critical moment.

One service is called Reporting Economic Crime Online (RECOL). It is an initiative that "… involves an integrated partnership between International, Federal and Provincial Law Enforcement agencies, as well as, with regulators and private commercial organizations that have a legitimate investigative interest in receiving a copy of complaints of economic crime. USER CONTROLLED CONSENT is required to direct fraud complaints to the appropriate law enforcement and regulatory agencies. RECOL will recommend the appropriate law enforcement or regulatory agency and/or private commercial organization for potential investigation. RECOL provides real time data pertaining to the current fraud trends. It also provides support for education, prevention and awareness of economic crime."

On-line help is available at https://www.recol.ca/login. aspx or call in service is also available at 1.888.495.8501.

Another Canadian service is called PhoneBusters (The Canadian Anti-Fraud Call Centre). It can be found at http://www.phonebusters.com/ and also reached Toll free: 1 888 495-8501, by Toll free fax: 1 888 654-9426 or via Email: info@phonebusters.com. This is a partnership of the RCMP, the Ontario Provincial Police, and Competition Bureau Canada.

By the way, Canada also has a Privacy Commission, which plays an important role in the discussion about personal identity.

"The mandate of the Office of the Privacy Commissioner of Canada (OPC) is overseeing compliance with both the Privacy Act, which covers the personal information-handling practices of federal government departments and agencies, and the Personal Information Protection and Electronic Documents Act (PIPEDA), Canada's private sector privacy law.

The mission of the Office of the Privacy Commissioner of Canada (OPC) is to protect and promote the privacy rights of individuals."

http://www.privcom.gc.ca/aboutUs/index_e.asp

This is a very interesting and important governmental institution because personal identity information should be regarded as a matter of constitutional privacy of the owner of the identity. This philosophy is closer to the European notion that identity is not a product, a commodity that can be harvested, bought, sold, and traded for money the way it is in the United States.

We wanted to share the following example about international identity risks. One of our colleagues is a world-renowned lecturer and author. In his travels in the Middle East, China, Europe, and other far-flung places, he has always worried about losing his passport or credit cards. He did in fact discover six months ago that one of his cards had unauthorized charges in Europe. The charges were substantial but covered by the card company's policy. Still, he worried about what other malicious things were being done with his card. He decided to purchase ID theft coverage. He chose Pre-Paid Legal Services, Inc. Two weeks ago he got a call from his ID theft company informing him of a suspicious charge. It turned out to be ok but he told us that just getting that call and knowing that his credit and other information was being constantly monitored was very reassuring and that it has been a great stress relief. A recent survey found that more Americans are worried about ID theft than about losing their jobs, so it's interesting that the "peace of mind" aspect of having insurance was very important to our colleague.

Americans rarely have the opportunity to think about the international implications and complications of identity theft risk and exposure. We hope that this brief review of Canadian initiatives and partnerships with the United States has been useful and informative.

In the following chapter we return to the US and examine detailed laws and policies to which US businesses must adhere. This does not constitute legal advice and you must consult with your attorneys for specific issues. The law is also constantly evolving so the information in Chapter 8 must be updated by consulting current publications.

CHAPTER 8
LAWS AND POLICIES FOR BUSINESS

In this book we have reviewed personal, corporate, and organizational responsibilities to secure data and personal information. We have also examined how you and corporations can and must develop defensive or protective measures to protect your identity, in addition to providing an analysis of some of the tools available to you.

One of the big problems is that government, including much of the federal government, is woefully behind the private sector and perhaps even the "evil doers" in the use of computers and information systems. Consider the following example of the lack of integration within government data systems.

"It is becoming increasingly apparent that having integrated information that is shared between various government agencies could make a huge difference in ongoing de-

tection and prevention of terrorist activity. It might have been able to change the outcome of the September 11th disaster. For example, two of the terrorists involved in the event were on an FBI watch list and, even though they boarded the flight using their real names, they weren't flagged by the airlines, airline security or others [1] [2]. This highlighted the issue that useful FBI watch list information is not shared appropriately with other enterprises such as airlines. The United States is one of the few countries that doesn't coordinate information between the Immigration Naturalization Service (INS) and the airports; thus, immigration and visa information often goes unnoticed by airlines. "National Intelligence and the Integration Gap: Terrorism: A Call for Data Integration," by Len Silverston, published in <u>DM Direct Newsletter, November 16, 2001</u>

The federal government is trying to fix this lack of data integration but suffered a big setback when the computer systems commissioned by the FBI proved to be so flawed that they are scrapping the whole thing and starting from scratch.

The role played by the 50 states and the federal government is indeed crucial to our identity security. As with any crime prevention, you need to have good locks on your doors, secure your purse and wallet, have well-lighted premises, put valuables in a safe place such as a bank safety deposit box, and use best practices in protecting yourself from crime. However, ultimately our safety varies on a day-to-day basis, depending on how many cops are on the beat, and how good the laws are that discourage or punish and lock up criminals. The role of government is the critical overall factor in making us safe against military or terrorist attacks, from crime, and safer from identity theft and identity crime.

As the following example demonstrates, the scale of ID theft information can be truly staggering.

The Problem -

"The theft of computer data at an Arizona company that put as many as 40 million credit card accounts at risk for fraud may have been the largest case of stolen consumer information yet.

But the incident, which was revealed last week and may have occurred months ago, surely will not be the last. In fact, the theft was only the latest in a series of incidents, not all of which involved criminal activity. Earlier this month, for example, United Parcel Service lost data tapes with personal information on nearly four million customers of Citigroup.

The problem of keeping data secure "exists on lots and lots of levels," said Marc Rotenberg, executive director of the Electronic Privacy Information Center in Washington. "You begin to see that the United States has an enormous problem that is spiraling out of control."

"Worry. But Don't Stress Out," by Henry Fountain, The New York Times, June 26, 2005, Section 4, p. 1.

The article goes on to point out that instead of a sudden catastrophic collapse of the system of electronic banking and commerce that drives the American economy, according to Mr. Fountain, "experts" agree that it will more likely be an on-going "creeping crisis." Its characteristics, he writes, are that as more and more information becomes digitized and networked, further intrusion and data losses will occur. In addition to financial data, more medical, educational, sports, and other data losses will take place. In this scenario, thieves will, for example, make many small illegal charges on stolen credit cards, which will be detected and corrected as they are discovered. However, this continuous violation may undermine confidence in electronic commerce and therefore hurt consumer confidence in the system, thus hurting the economy. Social Security numbers are also vulnerable to continuous, incremental theft and forgery. These can then be used as the credential for obtaining other documents, thus becoming "legitimate" by shifting identities to someone who is "clean." We call this process "Identity Laundering."

The presumption by Mr. Fountain of the New York Times (or his "experts" among which we are not since we were NOT consulted), that small, incremental problems are less serious than sudden and large ones is at best a weak argument and probably even an incorrect assumption.

Small incremental problems are often precisely the precursors to catastrophic ones. When an airplane crashes and the cause is determined to have been "metal fatigue" over many years, the consequences are no less deadly for the fact that it was coming slowly over a period of time. As Fountain himself metaphorizes, catastrophic earthquakes are most often the result of pressure building up at fault lines until the stress is so great that the fault yields.

So with credit card theft or more broadly identity theft, this continuous and accelerating nature is no reason for rejoicing. The cumulative effects of apprehension, consumer mistrust of major industries such as financial services, and the negative impact ID theft will have on e-commerce are certainly a reason to worry and to act.

We must be generally concerned about the continuous violation of personal information, the theft of credit card numbers, violations of medical records privacy, and bad practices in government management of citizen data (the use of "No child left behind" data including students' home phone numbers, data that was made available to military recruiters and who knows who else). In fact, periodically stories unfold that are truly incomprehensible.

In June of 2005, the story broke that the US Department of State had issued passports to people who were on Homeland Security Department Watch Lists, to criminals, drug dealers, identity thieves and others not entitled to US passports. The concern is not only with the general lack of appropriate cross-referencing of data in the Federal system, caused by an inept, turf-centered, uncoordinated, and antiquated bureaucracy. The much greater worry is that the number of ways in which the integrity and security of our personal identity can be violated keeps growing every week with new revelations. Moreover, it's bad enough that people are losing control over their credit cards and thus, potentially, their credit-worthiness. A passport allows the identity thief to travel, to enter the United States as a different person and, in these tense times, potentially use that cover to commit acts of terrorism.

No amount of airport security, screening, searches, bomb sniffing, or swiping baggage for explosives can correct for a fake identity. No amount of high level security threads, watermarks, laminated photographs, or even embedded digital information makes any difference if the wrong person has been certified to bear the passport.

As an important side bar, we should analyze briefly the new digital information that will be embedded in future passports. This data will be stored in a RFID device. This little chip is a transmitter that sends out a signal with whatever data has been programmed into it. Wal-Mart is also planning to put these into every future product in order to conduct continuous inventory control and other market/product data mining.

Embedded in passports, the device would transmit information about the identity of the person to whom the document was issued and this information is then received and read by a device the immigration officer has at her station. The idea is that as passengers enter the immigration area of the airport, the data will be transmitted and is available immediately for use by the authorities. This supposedly will save time, money, and also provide more security (we don't know how!).

The huge problem with RFID devices is that information is pervasively transmitted and not targeted like hard-wired information to a specific end user. Instead, like any radio signal, someone with a receiving device, anyone with a receiving device, may be able to capture the information and from what we know at this point can "virtually" harvest the identities of hundreds or thousands of passengers. Lack of experience and expertise, fascination with advanced technology, and a great big dose of naiveté may soon put at risk the personal identity of every person who owns a passport. Already the advice is that persons should wrap their passports in aluminum foil (preferably, one would presume, the heavy-weight barbeque grilling type) in order to suppress the signal. Entrepreneurs were reported to be developing designer "security pouches" (Sponge Bob Square Pants for kids and NASCAR or Tommy Hilfiger themes for adults?) which would shield the passport from the dangerous leakage of identity information.

This is another case of our government working against us. Again!

You might be asking yourself "is identity theft a federal crime?" Here is the information from the Federal Trade Commission.

Yes. **The Identity Theft and Assumption Deterrence Act** *is the main federal law directed at identity theft.*

The Act makes it a federal crime when someone:

"knowingly transfers or uses, without lawful authority, a means of identification of another person with the intent to commit, or to aid or abet, any unlawful activity that constitutes a violation of federal law, or that constitutes a felony under any applicable state or local law."

Note that under the Act, a name or SSN is considered a "means of identification." So is a credit card number, cellular telephone electronic serial number or any other piece of information that may be used alone or in conjunction with other information to identify a specific individual.

In most instances, a conviction for identity theft carries a maximum penalty of 15 years imprisonment, a fine and forfeiture of any personal property used or intended to be used to commit the crime. Schemes to commit identity theft or fraud also may involve violations of other statutes, such as credit card fraud; computer fraud; mail fraud; wire fraud; financial institution fraud; or Social Security fraud. Each of these federal offenses is a felony and carries substantial penalties - in some cases, as high as 30 years in prison, fines and criminal forfeiture.

In spite of this law, much more needs to happen at the federal and state levels to put teeth into legal identity protection. The following information provides an excellent overview of what can be done at the federal level. This material comes from California Senator Diane Feinstein and we thank her office for making this available. (The information has been edited and some material that is not germane to our book has been deleted).

What is striking about this material is that these hearings were held in the year 2000! As we all know, progress by the federal and state governments toward tightening and improving personal information has been at best weak. In fact, as we have demonstrated in this book, 2005 was the year when the most spectacular and astonishing data breaches occurred.

Definition of Identity Theft:

What is identity theft? Identity theft occurs when one person uses another person's Social Security number, birth date, driver's license number, or other identifying information to obtain credit cards, car loans, phone plans or other services in the victim's name.

Identity thieves can get personal information in a myriad of ways – stealing wallets and purses containing identification cards, using personal information found on the Internet, stealing mail (including pre-approved credit offers and credit statements), fraudulently obtaining credit reports or getting personnel records at work.

Identity theft has become a critical law enforcement issue:

• An identity is stolen every 60 seconds. As many as 700,000 incidents of identity theft will occur this year ;(source: Privacy Rights Clearinghouse).

• From 1997- 1999, there was a 380% increase in the reporting of Social Security number misuse;

• In a survey of 1000 Americans by Impulse Research of Los Angeles, 42 % of the respondents reported a member of their household had their personal identity or credit-card information stolen.

• Identity theft causes up to $3 billion in losses annually from credit card fraud alone.

Personal Impact of Identity Theft on Victims:

We will hear from two victims today who will describe the havoc to their lives caused by identity theft. Identity theft, unlike other crimes, is an ongoing crime that can last for years.

•   The typical victim of identity theft:

- Learns about the identity theft 14 months after it has occurred;

- Sustains $18,000 in fraudulent charges;

- and spends 175 hours over two years restoring their clean credit and good name.

Goal of the Hearing today:

Combating identity theft demands a coordinated effort. This hearing will explore how individuals can better protect themselves from fraud, and how the local and Federal governments can help put the clamps on identity theft.

1. The Federal government should make it harder to traffic in personally identifiable information;

2. Local law enforcement can increase the prosecution and investigation of identity theft; and

3. Individuals also can take preventive steps to protect themselves from identity thieves.

Federal Legislation:

There are very specific things the Federal government can do to aid in the fight against identity theft.

• Social Security number bill -

• First, we can cut down on the widespread traffic of the Social Security number.

• Social Security numbers are the prime tool used by identity thieves to capture victims' personal information and to set-up fraudulent credit card accounts.

• Today, on the Internet, an identity thief can buy another person's Social Security number for as little as $25 – no questions asked. This is simply wrong.

I have introduced the Social Security number Protection Act, which is endorsed by the Clinton-Gore Administration. This bill would prohibit the sale of a person's Social Security Number without their consent, except for a narrow number of circumstances such as law enforcement, national security, or public health purposes.

• Identity Theft Prevention Act -

• I have also introduced, the Identity Theft Prevention Act with my Senate colleagues John Kyl and Charles Grassley. This bill, which is endorsed by the Federal Trade Commission, offers a number of concrete, practical measures to cut-down criminal access to personal information and assist victims.

• For example, identity thieves often intercept bank statements or credit card statements and then redirect the account to another address. This bill would require credit issuers to notify the original cardholders at their original address of any address-change requests. Thus, cardholders will know any time a thief is trying to shift the address of his account.

• In addition, the bill would develop standardized forms for victims to report identity theft to banks credit bureaus and retail stores. Right now, identity theft victims typically have to fill out a new fraud report for each store with a fraudulent charge. Creating a standardized form could save many victims hundreds of hours of time of filling out redundant reports.

In summary, identity theft is a crime growing at alarming rates that deserves all of our attention. I look forward to hearing the reports and insights of the witnesses."

http://feinstein.senate.gov/releases00/identity_theft_
bill_hearing.html

Current Status of Federal and State Legislation on Identity Theft

There are several crucially important US federal laws that you need to know about which we will summarize for you. This information is very important for professionals, companies, organizations, as well as consumers.

1. The Identity Theft And Assumption Deterrence Act Of 1998

Although discussed above let's reiterate some of the

points. In October 1998, Congress passed the Identity Theft and Assumption Deterrence Act of 1998 (Identity Theft Act) to address the problem of identity theft. Specifically, the Act amended 18 U.S.C. § 1028 to make it a federal crime when anyone:

Knowingly transfers or uses, without lawful authority, a means of identification of another person with the intent to commit, or to aid or abet, any unlawful activity that constitutes a violation of Federal law, or that constitutes a felony under any applicable State or local law.

This legislation establishes the following procedures;

•   That the person whose identity was stolen is a true victim. Previously, only the credit grantors who suffered monetary losses were considered victims.

•   It enables the Secret Service, the Federal Bureau of Investigation, and other law enforcement agencies the authority to investigate this crime.

•   It allows the identity theft victim to seek restitution if there is a conviction.

•   It also establishes the Federal Trade Commission as a central agency to act as a clearinghouse for complaints, referrals, and resources for assistance for victims of identity theft.

The act is serious business and provides for the following punishment and penalties:

• Up to 15 years imprisonment in a Federal Penitentiary

• If convicted of Identity Theft, penalties of up to $250,000

2. Identity Theft Penalty Enhancement Act

The Identity Theft Penalty Enhancement Act was passed

by Congress to spell out penalties for those convicted of identity theft. Additionally, this act sets out penalties for those who possess information that can be used to perpetrate the crime of ID theft, regardless of whether or not these individuals themselves actually use the information to steal an identity. This tightening of the ID theft criteria is very significant because that type of personal confidential information is often sold to criminals who then commit ID theft.

According to the Library of Congress, section two of The Identity Theft Penalty Enhancement Act amends the Federal criminal code to establish penalties for "aggravated identity theft." Further it prescribes sentences to be imposed in addition to the punishments provided for the related felonies.

These additional punishments are:

1. Two years' imprisonment for knowingly transferring, possessing, or using, without lawful authority, a means of identification of another person during and in relation to specified felony violations (including theft of public property, theft by a bank officer or employee, theft from employee benefit plans, various fraud and immigration offenses, and false statements regarding Social Security and Medicare benefits).

2. Five years' imprisonment for knowingly taking such action with respect to a means of identification or a false identification document during and in relation to specified felony violations pertaining to terrorist acts. The act prohibits a court from:

• Placing any person convicted of such a violation on probation.

• Reducing any sentence for the related felony to take

into account the sentence imposed for such a violation.

• Providing for concurrent terms of imprisonment for a violation of this Act and a violation under any other Act.

Section three of the Act expands the existing identify theft prohibition to cover:

• Possession of a means of identification of another with intent to commit specified unlawful activity.

• Increase penalties for violations to include acts of domestic terrorism within the scope of a prohibition against facilitating an act of international terrorism.

Section Six authorizes appropriations to the Department of Justice for the investigation and prosecution of identity theft and related credit card and other fraud cases constituting felonies.

These are just a few of the sections under the Act. This is a robust tightening of the Act and is a signal that finally the feds are getting serious about ID theft.

2. FACTA - New Fair and Accurate Credit Transactions Act

The Fair and Accurate Credit Transactions Act of 2003 (FACTA) is a United States federal law, passed by Congress on December 4, 2003. It is an amendment to the Fair Credit Reporting Act. FACTA allows consumers to request and obtain a free credit report once every twelve months from each of the three US consumer credit reporting companies (Equifax, Experian and TransUnion). In cooperation with the Federal Trade Commission, the three major credit reporting agencies set up the website, www.annualcreditreport.com, to provide free access to annual credit reports.

FACTA also contains provisions to help reduce identity theft, such as the ability for individuals to place alerts on their credit histories if identity theft is suspected, or if deploying overseas in the military. These provisions make fraudulent applications for credit more difficult. FACTA also requires secure disposal of sensitive consumer information. "Reasonable measures" of destruction include:

Burning, pulverizing or shredding documents so they become impossible to read or put back together.

Erasing electronic files or media files that contain any consumer reports so that they cannot be recovered or reconstructed.

After auditing to ensure their practices are sufficient and guaranteed to be successful, you can also hire an outside source who is proficient in the destruction of personal records.

The Fair and Accurate Credit Transactions Act also affects small business by limiting the amount of information that can be printed on a credit or debit card receipt. Beginning January 1, 2005, all newly purchased credit card machines print only the last five digits of the credit card number.

Another key item in FACTA was the requirement that mortgage lenders provide consumers with a Credit Disclosure Notice that included their credit scores, range of scores, credit bureaus, scoring models, and factors affecting their scores. This form is available from credit reporting agencies, and many will send this directly to the consumer on the lenders' behalf.

FACTA also has a "Red Flag Rule" which requires a financial institution or creditor that maintains "covered accounts" to develop a written Identity Theft Prevention Program to detect, prevent, and mitigate identity theft.

Under the final regulations of the Red Flag rule there are four basic elements that must be included in the Program:

• *Identify relevant Red Flags for covered accounts and incorporate those Red Flags into the Program;*

• *Detect Red Flags that have been incorporated into the Program;*

• *Respond appropriately to any Red Flags that are detected to prevent and mitigate identity theft; and*

• *Ensure the Program is updated periodically, to reflect changes in risks to customers or to the safety and soundness of the financial institution or creditor from identity theft.*

The full recent Red Flag Rule is available from the FTC at this address: http://www.ftc.gov/os/2007/10/r611019redflagsfrn.pdf

The Regulation also expands on the steps that financial institutions and creditors must take to administer above rules.

   * *Approval of the initial written Program by the board of directors or a committee of the board,*

   * *ensuring oversight of the program;*

   * *training of relevant staff;and*

   * *overseeing provider arrangements*

The Program must be appropriate to the size and complexity of the financial institution or creditor and the nature and scope of its activity.

3. HIPPA

According to the Department of Health and Human Services, "The first-ever federal privacy standards to protect patients' medical records and other health information provided to health plans, doctors, hospitals and other health care providers took effect on April 14, 2003. Developed by the Department of Health and Human Services (HHS), these standards (the Privacy Rule) provide patients with access to their medical records and more control over how their personal health information is used and disclosed. They represent a uniform, federal floor of privacy protections for consumers across the country. State laws providing additional protections to consumers are not affected by this rule."

The Health Insurance Portability and Accountability Act of 1996 (HIPAA) is a good example of the serious effort being undertaken by the federal government to wall off personal and confidential information of medical patients. If you have been to a doctor recently, you will no doubt have signed a HIPPA form as part of your checking in procedure.

According to the Department of HHS

HIPAA included provisions designed to encourage electronic transactions and also required new safeguards to protect the security and confidentiality of health information. Health plans, health care clearinghouses, and those health care providers who conduct certain financial and administrative transactions (e.g., enrollment, billing and eligibility verification) electronically are required to comply with the provisions of the Privacy Rule. HHS has conducted extensive outreach and provided guidance and technical assistant to these providers and businesses to make it as easy as possi-

ble for them to implement the privacy protections established through the Privacy Rule. These efforts include answers to hundreds of common questions about the rule, as well as explanations and descriptions about key elements of the rule.

If you need more details or have questions, these materials are available at http://www.hhs.gov/ocr/hipaa.

4. GLBA Compliance

Full Compliance with the Gramm-Leach-Bliley Safeguard Rule (Gramm Leach Bliley Act - GLBA) means that a company has to establish a system for " ... providing an initial notice to all new customers, have mailed the initial notices to all existing customers and have afforded them the opportunity to opt out of any disclosures which are not otherwise permitted by law." GLBA is also known as the Financial Services Modernization Act of 1999. It provides limited privacy protections against the sale of consumers' private financial information. GLBA also codifies protections against pretexting, which is the practice of obtaining personal information through false pretenses.

GLBA's privacy protections only regulate financial institutions, businesses that are engaged in banking, insuring, stocks and bonds, financial advice, and investing.

To be within GLB/GLBA Compliance, a company must also have procedures and policies in place to ensure that **Non-Public Personal Information (NPI)** is safeguarded, kept, transferred and disposed of in a "confidential manner."

ID Theft at the US State Level

If any of you have doubted why those wise founders of

the Republic devised federalism, identity theft yields one compelling clue. States can innovate and devise advanced policies that address issues the Federal government has neglected. We have shared with you the case of Hawaii earlier in this book. However, California is often the lead state in devising new regulations, new policies, new solutions, and new ways of dealing with serious problems. They are often the precursor for what is going to happen in 5 or 10 years in other states.

Starting in 2002, California began seriously tightening up identity protection.

Of course, California, in some ways, is not a state but really a country! If California's economic size were measured by itself against other countries, it would rank as having the 7th largest economy in the world. California is the biggest state economy in the United States, and one out of every eight United States residents lives in California.

In the area of identity theft, California has been a pioneer in the nation. The state passed strict laws that require extensive reporting of identity theft by corporations, strict penalties for impostors who misuse a person's identity, and requires actions by credit bureaus to block use of a person's hijacked credit. These bureaus must also issue security alerts in a timely manner when they have a breach.

California, therefore, has pushed identity protection much further than the federal government or any other state (although almost all states have ID theft laws of some sort today). The revelations of serious security breaches in 2005 were largely thanks to the California identity report laws.

Since ID theft laws are moving targets, evolving and constantly morphing, we suggest that you look at the **Federal Trade Commission** web site, which has a good summary of these laws. http://www.consumer.gov/idtheft/federallaws. html#criminalstate

U.S. Senate Republican leaders finally tipped their hand Thursday on long-awaited identity-theft legislation. After months of back room maneuvering, the proposed bill is likely to provoke howls of protest from both the technology and financial services industries.

The Identity Theft Protection Act (S.B. 1408), co-sponsored by Senate Commerce Committee Chairman Ted Stevens (R-Alaska) and Hawaiian Democrat Daniel Inouye, the ranking member of the Commerce Committee, requires companies, government agencies and educational institutions to disclose to consumers breaches of both encrypted and unencrypted data and imposes fines of up to $11 million for violators.

"The fear out there is real and is something we must deal with as quickly as possible," said Stevens at a Washington press conference....

This legislation will require that organizations holding sensitive personal information secure it with physical and technological safeguards that will be specified by the Federal Trade Commission (FTC). The bill applies to any business, school, or other entity that collects information (Social Security numbers, financial account information, driver's license information and other information that the FTC determines can be used for identity theft). The bill also applies to any third party that buys or acquires this type of information.

If any information is lost, hacked, or compromised, the

entity is required to report it to the person whose data has been taken within a maximum of 90 days.

Harris Miller, president of the Information Technology Association of America (ITAA), has objected to parts of this new legislation, arguing that data that has been encrypted or otherwise "protected" from unauthorized users should be exempt from notification requirements, which would cost the industry millions of dollars.

Under the new federal bill, identity-theft victims could put a freeze on their credit reports, a move that is strongly opposed by the financial services industry.

Representative Joe Barton (R-Texas), chairman of the Energy and Commerce Committee, will introduce a similar bill in the House, which reminds us that it may still be a long time before we have a new ID theft bill at the federal level.

Although a new law would be useful, the entire culture of the federal government needs to be overhauled; old-line, turf conscious bureaucrats need to be fired (almost impossible because of Civil Service protection), retired, seriously retrained, or transferred because in many cases they are impeding the implementation of new policies to protect, especially against cyber crime (Internet and information technology-based problems). Consider the following comments on the performance of the Federal Cyber Corps, created to bring modern, high-tech data and security to government agencies.

Federal administrators are overhauling Cyber Corps because conflicting policies and management structures are making it increasingly difficult to place graduates of the infosec training program in government jobs. University co-

ordinators say getting the first 50 Cyber Corps graduates into federal jobs proved extremely difficult. Federal agencies were unwilling to hire inexperienced security admins when more senior infosec positions went unfilled. Complicating the situation is the Office of Personnel Management (OPM), which is responsible for placing students but has little authority to compel placements. "I don't pretend to understand how government works," says Douglas Jacobson, an Iowa State professor who advises 22 program participants. "I don't even know whom to blame, but there's clearly a problem here. The people doing the hiring don't seem to have a stake in the process."

CYBER CORPS' FAILING GRADES. Federal officials are revamping the infosec training program to resolve critical job placement problems, by Vin McLellan, June 2003, http://infosecuritymag.techtarget.com/2003/jun/cybercorps. shtml

To the best of our knowledge, by January of 2008 the problem has not improved much.

We are very well aware of this problem since some of our brightest and most talented students in information security waited and finally gave up on receiving federal security clearances and instead accepted jobs from private sector firms. Not that this is a bad thing – we need them in the private sector very badly! However, the federal government is the most effective force in bringing cybercrime and identity thieves to their knees and improving our personal identity security.

The time has come for a major initiative – we call it an **ID Theft Marshall Plan**, after the massive effort post WW II to rebuild Europe. Congress and the President need to take a bold and affirmative initiative in this area and work closely with the private sector to change the security paradigm once and for all and give the good guys, the white hats, the upper hand.

Until that happens, batten down your hatches, be identity smart, don't leave stuff lying around, freeze your credit rating if that fits your lifestyle, and for goodness sake sign up for one of the good identity theft protection plans that can help you protect yourself. Here is an even better idea, give your mom or dad or your kids an annual identity theft protection plan for Christmas. You could not give a more helpful gift!

We should note here that as we have indicated earlier, none of this information should be construed as legal advice. That can only be obtained from your attorney or the attorney for your identity theft protection plan. Since many readers are interested in or have an ID theft protection service, we felt that it would be useful to review comparatively the products on the market. We do this in Chapter 9.

CHAPTER 9

PRODUCT COMPARISON

"One of our Pre-Paid Legal Services, Inc.'s Life Events Legal Plan ˢᴹ member received notice of a court hearing for a speeding ticket. The member did not recall ever having received a speeding ticket so she contacted Wagner, Falconer & Judd, Ltd. As part of the member's Motor Vehicle Legal Expense Services (Title 2) benefits, an attorney discussed the member's situation and agreed to go to court with her. Once in court it was argued that the member had not in fact been cited for speeding but that the ticket must have belonged to someone else. The prosecutor repeatedly refused to dismiss the ticket until the member and the Title 2 attorney had made a third court appearance. Finally, during the third court appearance, the Title 2 attorney was able to convince the prosecutor to compare the booking photos of the individual cited for speeding to the member and it was discovered that the photos did not match our member's appearance. We believe that the individual cited for speeding was the member's sister though that was never proven. Regardless, once the

prosecutor was convinced that the booking photos did not match the member's appearance, he agreed to dismiss the speeding charge against her."

Pre-Paid Legal Services, Inc.
Provider Law Firm, Minnesota

CONSIDER THESE FACTS:

According to the Federal Trade Commission, nearly 10 million Americans fell victim to identity theft last year, at an average cost of $5,000 per victim. The actual numbers vary quite a bit and there are estimates far greater than this because many ID theft victims never report the crime for various reasons – for example, people with dubious residency status in the US or Canada, people who themselves have outstanding warrants even just for speeding tickets - are afraid of the authorities. But two-thirds of victims who discovered the misuse of their personal information within five months incurred **no out-of-pocket expenses**. That's what a credit monitoring service can do for you - it can't prevent identity theft, but it can greatly reduce its impact.

Be careful because some companies only reimburse their clients for the expenses incurred in trying to **recover their identities,** not the replacement costs of actual thefts and financial losses that happen when thieves misuse their Social Security cards or other identification documents.

Credit card companies normally cover the abuse of their cards by unauthorized users. Make sure that in addition to checking the interest rates and other benefits that vary from card to card - free travel, loss insurance, life and limb insurance, rental car coverage, funeral transfer expenses of the deceased back to their homes – you find out what the policy is on covering losses from fraudulent use of your card. Most are regulated by federal law, so there should not be great differences between credit card companies and banks. You must understand what your credit card company's policy is regarding fraudulent charges before you open the account.

The latest data we were able to review shows that credit card companies are improving their security regime by, for example, not authorizing suspicious looking transactions (a Ferrari rental in Italy, 3 Rolex watches at a Rio de Janeiro jewelry store, and 3 nights at a luxury spa in Hawaii all on the same day!) and/or by notifying the card holder to verify charges. So credit card losses are down even as identity theft/fraud protection services are on the rise.

One interesting development is the arrival on the market of insurance style identity theft policies and other identity fraud protection services. Many of these products and services are sold directly to consumers and they include such services as credit monitoring, fraud alerts, data mining, 24/7 access to attorneys, and most recently, credit freezes.

*A **fraud alert** is another tool for people who've had their ID stolen – or who suspect it may have been stolen. With a fraud alert in place, businesses may still check your credit report. Depending on whether you place an initial 90-day fraud alert or an extended fraud alert, potential creditors must either contact you or use what the law refers to as "reasonable policies and procedures" to verify your identity before issuing credit in your name. However, the steps potential creditors take to verify your identity may not always alert them that the applicant is not you.*

FTC - Fighting Back Against Identity Theft
The identity theft protection service industry has expe-

rienced double-digit growth in the last few years alone with no end in sight. This growth is a product of the justifiable fear on the part of consumers that they are at risk. One of the problems that accompany this concern with ID theft is that experts agree that there are too many "fly-by-night" companies selling ID theft products and only a hand full of companies that have multiple years of experience.

In this chapter we have prepared a short comparative analysis of four of the top companies in the industry by name recognition only or by services offered. The four firms are Equifax, LifeLock, Pre-Paid Legal Services Inc, and State Auto Insurance.

Incidentally, we feel confident that identity theft insurance/services will be as common in the near future as car insurance, homeowners insurance, medical insurance, and life insurance are today. After all, our grandparents had none of these but as times changed, the extended family disappeared and as we have now faced new economic, technological and social realities, we've had to protect ourselves with services and insurance.

It is not just the money and time that burden consumers who suffer ID theft losses. President Bush created The President's Task Force on Identity Theft, which was established by Executive Order 13402 on May 10, 2006. The information from the White House states that "Recognizing the heavy financial and emotional toll that identity theft exacts from its victims, and the severe burden it places on the economy, President Bush called for a coordinated approach among government agencies to combat this crime."

We have not found a reliable measure of the emotional costs of being a victim of ID theft but it surely takes its toll on the health and personal happiness of victims. So the best advice we've found from experts is that prevention is the best strategy, as it is with heart disease, cholesterol, obesity, and other health problems. The equivalent of regular exercise, a healthy diet, and stress relief is clearly practicing "safe identity protection" as a consumer and having insurance coverage since it is likely, with the explosion of data mining and data breaches, that you will suffer some sort of "identity compromised" event sometime in your life.

Maxine Sweet, VP of public education at Experian, one of the largest credit reporting agencies has said that "There's no one who can do it [monitor, defend, and recover their identity information] other than the consumer." Yes, they're victims. Yes, it's a terrible crime. But there's no one else who can do it." We respectfully disagree. It's like saying that when your health deteriorates, there is no one except you who can improve your health.

Another theory is that government should take care of this problem. While we agree that laws and regulations regarding the protection of your confidential personal information should be tightened, the government cannot take care of every person's identity information loss. First of all, it is doubtful that consumers would be willing to shell out in taxes what it would cost to have government run such programs. Second of all, the government itself has a terrible track record protecting confidential information as we have demonstrated in several places in this book (the loss of 25 million military records being a spectacular example of this). Americans have never been comfortable with the idea of the government providing all health , home and disaster insurance, and certainly not car insurance.

The most reasonable solution to ID theft is to have the private sector compete with a range of different products. This has always been the most effective way to have the demand by consumers for identity theft protection services met with the supply of such products. In the competition that ensues, there will be (and there already are today) a wide range of approaches to satisfying this consumer need at various price ranges and with different solutions.

Insurance is only one of the ways that this need for ID and financial theft protection can be addressed. The market economy likes this model because insurance is based on a calculation of risk and cost. Consumers buy insurance at a price that allows the company to furnish such a service, make an appropriate profit, and stay in business to continue providing this service over a person's lifetime and beyond. Insurance is also heavily regulated and therefore subject to a variety of criteria on best practice and ethical business behavior, which affords the consumer significant protection in normal times. By aggregating the collective insurance premiums and only having to spend on clients who actually suffer losses, the industry can reduce the costs of individual premiums since this is a form of "pooled risk costs."

Remember, identity theft is fairly new as an insurable loss and the traditional insurance company's actuaries are only now designing models of how to estimate the pending losses their clients may experience. This is one reason that the traditional insurance option is such a troubling one. Not only do "traditional" insurers have no idea how likely you are to experience identity theft, they have no reliable way of estimating the cost of your theft experience. Identity theft as a crime is still too new for longitudinal, historical data to answer these traditional questions.

Some traditional insurance companies are developing and offering ID theft policies as add-ons for their current customers. Often this type of coverage is a rider on a homeowner policy and sits next to wind, fire, water, liability, and other risks that are covered. Huck Jaffe from MarketWatch wrote a Dec. 5, 2006, column titled "Stupid Investment of the Week: Identity-theft insurance isn't even worth its small price." Here was his comment on traditional insurance:

Some people like carrying both an umbrella and a raincoat, figuring they can never be too well covered in the event of a storm. When it comes to insuring against a serious problem like identity theft, any consumer who is worried about the issue is most likely taking the raincoat and umbrella steps. Purchasing insurance is kind of like adding an extra poncho and a tarp; it's unlikely to be necessary, will provide minimal extra protection and could be a hassle to open during a storm. And that's why the identity-theft insurance policies offered by many leading homeowners companies are a Stupid Investment of the Week.

He goes on to point out that typical homeowners insurance "… pays for repairs and damages, or replaces something that has been lost. If your house or car is damaged, insurance goes a long way to fixing the problem."

Identity theft, however, is not the loss of something that you can go and replace at Home Depot. Instead, identity-theft cases, Jaffe correctly explains, the damages, is something like a ruined credit record or the ID thieves may ruin your reputation and name by committing crimes as YOU. So what does the traditional insurance identity policy cover? Credit card losses? No, because credit card companies already cover illegal and criminal charges to your credit card. Instead they offer you reimbursements, from $10 to $25,000 depending on the policy, for expenses related to certified mail, phone calls, and other direct costs you incur in trying to fix your ID theft problem. Jaffe and others also point out that these policies do not involve protective and preventive activities (such as monitoring services) that will either prevent or reduce the impact of an identity theft "break in" into your personal information. He also notes that often they do not include any legal fees or other real costs that ID theft victims will incur.

The next obvious question is whether average consumers are willing to pay a monthly fee to assist them in protecting their personal information. This is a question that Professor James McQuivey of Boston University's College of Communication and a handful of graduate students attempt to answer in their research shared in our previous book "Who Is You; The Coming Epidemic of Identity Theft." The following is an excerpt from that question.

"Will Americans pay to protect their personal information? It's a question insurance companies want the answer to so they can decide just what to offer people. And it's a question I tackled at Boston University's College of Communication where I teach. We conducted an online survey of 1,049 adults in the U.S. with sample provided by Survey Sampling International. Our goal was first to see how much of a problem people perceived identity theft was and then see if people

were willing to pay to protect themselves against it.

Four in five Americans agree that identity theft is "a major problem in the United States." Nearly a third of us – 31% – are very concerned that identity theft will happen to us in the next five years. And when offered the option to pay for an insurance policy that would take care of their credit history, bank accounts and credit accounts in the event their identity was stolen, 72% indicated they were willing to pay at least something.

However, what most of the industry is prepared to provide is reimbursement for expenses incurred in restoring your credit: mailing costs, notary cost, long distance phone costs, even including lost wages for some policies. Yet remember the emotional toll described by people who experience identity theft. Can an insurance policy designed to reimburse you for taking weeks out of your life to restore your good name actually make you feel better? - James McQuivey

It seems to us that companies that continue to hang their hats on policies that offer you a $15,000 or $25,000 reimbursement for out of pocket expenses simply do not have a true understanding of the new and identity-theft specific industry that has been emerging nor do they have an understanding of what the victims might be experiencing. As mentioned in McQuivey's earlier article, these reimbursements often cover costs for notary fees, mailing costs, lost income, and charges for long distance phone calls. Well, quite frankly, that is a lot of 41¢ stamps!

The true aggravation and cost to a victim of the crime of identity theft is the feeling of being alone, vulnerable, and frustrated with the steps it takes and the time it consumes to rectify the problem, along with the feeling of being violated. This is on top of the fact that you will spend countless hours repairing the damage only to find out a year, a few months, or even days later you have become a victim again.

Just as any good free market should do, the United States and Canada have opened the doors for numerous companies to fill the obvious gap that exists between the product the traditional homeowner insurance industry is offering and what the public actually needs.

We have done a simple comparative assessment between four different companies of some of these products, which is summarized on *page 190-191 table.*

One of the companies in the table is Pre-Paid Legal Services Inc, an Ada, Oklahoma based corporation, traded on the NYSE. This company has partnered with Kroll Worldwide to create a variety of services that address the identity theft problem. Pre-Paid Legal Services sees not only a market opportunity in this ever growing industry of identity theft but also a way to make a relevant and problem-appropriate difference in their clients' lives.

One observer noted that Pre-Paid Legal seem to have looked at the problem of identity theft and asked themselves, "What if, instead of simply paying people back (like most reactive, traditional insurance style products) for the work they had to do, we actually took over the work of restoring their credit and legal issues for them?"

If you can gain access to a company with trained experts in resolving credit and legal problems quickly and efficiently who are equipped to apply these skills to thousands of individuals simultaneously, you have a powerful force in your corner. If it happens to be a company that has been in business for over 30 years, it's icing on the cake. That's what it seems Pre-Paid Legal Services Inc. has accomplished with their Life Events Legal Plan SM and their Legal Shield included with their Identity Theft product.

Although the service provided by Pre-Paid Legal runs around $360 annually per couple, it is clearly the 800 pound gorilla in the room on ID theft protection. This product can be purchased individually or delivered in other insurance-like channels. For example, it can be offered as either an employee fringe benefit or a voluntary employee benefit. It would be our recommendation to upper-management and human resource directors to add such a product to the benefit package. Not only would this make a person a more loyal employee, it would save the employer from losing productivity during the weeks and months that employees with identity theft problems are preoccupied with fixing their problems.

Pre-Paid Legal Services Inc's two tiered solution, Life Events Legal Plan SM and the Legal Shield combined with the Identity Theft Shield seems to be the next step in the evolution of identity theft prevention services. Pre-Paid Legal Services has access to top ranked attorneys within a closed network giving its members access before, during and after becoming victims of identity theft, twenty four hours seven days a week. In our opinion and in the opinion of many of our colleagues and other experts, this is the direction in which the entire industry must move.

It is a cliché to say that bad things happen to good people without discrimination in regards to age, sex, religion, or financial class. Robust identity protection and recovery products are really the only way to be intelligently prepared for a potential hit.

In order to bring closer to home the issue of ID theft and ID protection we have asked Lt Colonel Travis Acheson to share his experience with us. The following piece was written exclusively for this book.

With more and more of our brave soldiers traveling halfway around the world to protect our freedom, the faceless crime of identity theft adds another twist to our story. The following letter by Lt. Colonel Travis Acheson, an F-16 fighter pilot with the US Armed Forces, makes that point abundantly clear.

Dear Michael McCoy,

Subject: Pro-Active Preparation - Both at Home and Abroad

I know first hand what it takes to prepare for war - lining up coworkers to take over your civilian job responsibilities, making sure your life insurance coverage is sufficient, meeting with the attorneys to ensure your will is updated, and saying goodbye to your wife and kids. As I prepare for the fifth time to deploy overseas to fly combat support missions in Operation Iraqi Freedom, I have learned you cannot do enough to prepare yourself and your family.

While serving, especially in combat situations, our job related task takes top priority. Organizing finances, taking care of personal issues, and even getting the daily mail can be a challenge. When you're fighting in a war, you don't have time to worry about day to day problems that could be affecting your family's household, let alone what could be happening with your personal information. But with a history of hackers gaining access to the computer systems of Bank of America, where approximately 1.2 million service members had their personal information compromised, I know it's a problem I can't ignore. Especially because as a military member, I am required to carry a Bank of America government credit card to cover all food and travel expenses.

In the military, we are identified by our name, rank and "serial number." We carry our serial number (Social Security number) on our military ID cards and dog tags. We are prime targets for identity theft. Family members of those serving have even been known to give out personal information to criminals presenting themselves as military officers.

Another issue facing military members placed in harm's way is having a current will. While statistics show that more than 70% of all families do not have a last will and testament, I won't make that mistake. Regardless of my deployment status, it would be a grave mistake not to properly protect my wife and family by having an updated will on file.

I chose to be proactive and I chose to be smart. But while an updated last will and testament to protect my family is a must, it does not have to break the bank. And I wouldn't even know where to call to find a good attorney. With a number of programs on the market today (and there are lots), I picked the most complete solution at a price I could afford. I found the industry leading program to be Pre-Paid Legal Services, Inc. They offer both the Life Events Legal Plan and the Iden-

tity Theft Shield. The last thing I want to do is react to an identity theft crisis when I get home in a few months. When purchased together, at the cost of less than one dollar per day, my family has complete protection and peace of mind.

Think about it...at less than one dollar per day I can have access to the best legal attorneys across the country, 24 hours a day. Even when I am deployed overseas, my wife can call our family attorney whether she has a simple legal question or a more complicated matter to deal with. We each had our wills completed at the local law office, including medical power of attorney and a living will. And updates every year cost nothing extra - it's part of the program. The Life Events Legal Plan when combined with the Identity Theft Shield, provide me and my wife with daily credit monitoring and restoration by Kroll, an industry leader. It's a comprehensive program, whether I'm in the great USA or half a world away.

Securing my family, our legal rights, and our identity helps provide me peace of mind.

You can't put a price tag on that.

LTC Travis Acheson

F-16 Pilot - Iowa Air National Guard

We have covered the nature of ID theft, what personal identity is and how we acquire it, what the general forms of ID theft are, and how to protect against these crimes. In the following chapter we take a peek into the future.

Identity Theft Service Comparison

	LifeLock	Pre-Paid Legal Services, Inc.	Equifax Credit Watch Gold ™	State Auto Insurance
	www.lifelock.com	www.prepaidlegal.com	www.equifax.com	www.stateauto.com
Overall Rating:	Medium Low Semi-Proactive	High Proactive	Medium Proactive	Low Reactive
Cost:	$20.00/mo per couple	$29.95/mo per couple	1st month free, $25.90 per couple	Provided to all State Auto home and farm insurance customers
Product Type	Service	Service	Service	Traditional Insurance
Credit bureau data source:	Equifax | Experian | TransUnion	Equifax | Experian | TransUnion	Equifax | Experian | TransUnion	None
Most Notable Feature:	$1,000,000 guarantee	Most Robust with access to attorneys 24/7 and complete restoration and credit monitoring.	Unlimited Equifax reports	It is included with your existing home or farm policy. Carries a $250 deductible
Overview and Recommendation	You can do everything they do on your own very easily. One of the least expensive non insurance company products on the market. It locks your ability to obtain instant credit which is a pro and a con.	More expensive but when the two products are packaged together, it is by far the most robust program on the market. Includes all traditional IDT services with access to legal counsel 24/7 (IDT is NOT only financial)	Good product. However, there is a slight problem that the exact companies (credit repositories) that are causing many of the problems are actually selling products to cover the very losses they are contributing to.	Very reactive policy. People should not use this option as their sole option. If an insurance company is going to offer it as a free benefit, you should treat it as such and still carry a proactive style product from another provider.

Service features and pricing verified as accurate on 24 January 2008 through individual websites. The table reflects our research and is solely our opinion. This information should be investigated by consumers prior to their choosing the right product that fits their personal needs or those of their families.

	Details	Details	Details	Details
Credit score included:	Yes	Yes	Yes	No
I.D. Theft Expense Reimbursement Coverage:	Yes – 1,000,000	No	Yes - $20,000	Yes - $15,000
Credit analysis tools:	No	Yes	No	No
Credit bureau data source:	Equifax | Experian | TransUnion	Equifax | Experian | TransUnion	Equifax | Experian | TransUnion	Equifax | Experian | TransUnion
Easy to ready credit report:	Good	Excellent	Good	Neutral
Frequency of credit alerts:	They have placed a credit alert on your credit file so you can not get instant credit	Every business day (via e-mail or mail)	Every business day (via e-mail, phone, mail or text messaging)	Only available after you become a victim
New credit report available:	Annually	Yes – periodically	Yes - periodically	After you become a victim
Credit alerts report:	- new accounts - credit inquiries - address changes - public records - changes to current accounts	- new accounts - credit inquiries - address changes - public records - changes to account info	- new accounts - credit inquiries - address changes - public records to current accounts	-NA
Company owned by:	LifeLock	Pre-Paid Legal Services Inc.	Equifax	State Auto Insurance service administered by Identity Theft 911™

CHAPTER 10
THE FUTURE

"Scenario One: After the Storm, Reform"

"There's no need to imagine a worst-case scenario for Internet security in the year 2010. The worst-case scenario is unfolding right now. Based on conservative projections, we'll discover about 100,000 new software vulnerabilities in 2010 alone, or one new bug every five minutes of every hour of every day. The number of security incidents worldwide will swell to about 400,000 a year, or 8,000 per workweek. The Windows operating system will approach 100 million lines of code, and the average [Personal Computer], while it may cost $99, will contain nearly 200 million lines of code. And within that code, 2 million bugs. By 2010, we'll have added another half-a-billion users to the Internet. A few of them will be bad guys, and they'll be able to pick and choose which of those 2 million bugs they feel like exploiting.

In other words, today's sloppiness will become tomorrow's chaos.

http://www.computerworld.com/
printthis/2003/0,4814,88646,00.html

Did we scare the pants off you with this!?

No worries say the authors of this Computerworld scenario. The worst will probably not happen because there is now a real awareness that Internet security is vitally important. Software companies and computer manufacturers will supposedly address this very frightening problem which has profoundly troubling implications for identity security but also more generally the security of proprietary information at companies as well as the national security of states.

IT security and especially security on the World Wide Web is the key to protecting the United States from external "cyber attacks" and it is one of the critical components of securing and defending your personal identity security and that of the 300 million other Americans, Canadians, Europeans, and others who have become vulnerable to cyber crime.

We have seen, much to our chagrin, the vulnerability of all forms of identification currently used in the United States. We have also demonstrated the risks in using credit cards, the currency of the United States (oh, sorry, the US dollar is technically the official currency, but of course paper money is used less and less every day, so technically Visa and Master Card are the currency of the United States).

So where does this leave us if we are to get relief from the terrible stress caused by bad identification methods and a rapidly increasing threat of identity theft?

There are numerous alternatives in the works and we will walk you through a few of them in this chapter.

VeriChip is an interesting approach to identity. Although it sounds like a new snack food, it's in fact one of the several high tech solutions rapidly coming on the market. This is a small capsule a little bigger than a grain of rice. It is implanted just under the skin with a quick, simple and painless procedure. Once implanted, the VeriChip can be scanned when necessary with a VeriChip scanner. The big selling point is that VeriChip can't be lost, stolen, misplaced, or counterfeited.

This is one of the identification systems that has both gotten a lot of buzz and also, of course, been the target of intense criticism by civil liberties groups. In truth, having an id tag implanted like our dogs have, is not such a secure identification system at all. Experts argue that criminals or terrorists can get hold of the equipment necessary to create an ID capsule, enter false ID data, implant them in themselves, and BINGO, they are you (or anyone else they want to be)!

An anti-chip group in fact made the following information available on January 27, 2006 with a headline that read "VERICHIP RFID IMPLANT HACKED!"and went on to say:

"This revelation along with other worrisome details could put a crimp in VeriChip Corporation's planned initial public offering (IPO) of its common stock, say Katherine Albrecht and Liz McIntyre. The anti-RFID [Radio Frequency Identification Device] activists and authors of "Spychips: How Major Corporations and Government Plan to Track Your Every Move with RFID" make no bones about their objection to VeriChip's plans to inject glass encapsulated RFID tags into people. But now they've discovered information that could call VeriChip's entire business model into question.

"If you look at the VeriChip purely from the business an-

gle, it's a ridiculously flawed product," says McIntyre. She notes that security researcher Jonathan Westhues has shown how easy it is to clone a VeriChip implanted in a person's arm and program a new chip with the same number."

Spychips.com, "VERICHIP RFID IMPLANT HACKED! Will Security Problems Quash IPO Plans for Controversial Company?"

http://www.spychips.com/press-releases/verichip-hacked.html

Besides "The Chip" there are many other and hopefully less controversial suggested improvements in personal ID security.

Fingerprints and hand palm prints have been used all over the world but much less so in the United States, where getting finger printed is often equated to being arrested and brought into the criminal justice system. Fingerprints are one of the most ancient and still fairly reliable forms of telling one person apart from another. Anyone who watches movies or TV will be quite familiar with the elaborate capabilities of law enforcement to read and match even just partial fingerprints. Fingerprint reading and matching devices have been embedded in many computer security pads. There is also a commercially used pay-by-fingerprint device that can be found, for example, in grocery stores. Once you've signed up for it, the device allows you to pay by simply sticking your finger on a pad and then entering a short id PIN number that you have set.

The federal government and Homeland Security have been working on advanced secure drivers' licenses called

Real ID. REAL ID Act is a federal law that is supposed to make it more difficult for terrorists, illegal immigrants and others to get official identification. State ID cards and drivers' licenses are easy to obtain and even forge. Background checks for drivers' licenses would be enhanced and standardized throughout the US. and would be printed much like US currency, on very secure paper, with extensive use of watermarks, security threads, special inks, secure lamination, photographs that look like the person, and even more high tech biometric information.

Detractors argue that the new license does not solve the age-old problem of verifying documentation against an individual flesh and blood identity. The LA Times ran an opinion piece by Jon Healey on January 22, 2008, which said in part;

"The biggest of those flaws [with the new licenses] is the tenuous link between identity verification and security. As security expert Bruce Schneier told the Senate Judiciary Committee last year, "A reliance on ID cards is based on a dangerous security myth: the idea that if only we knew who everyone was, we could pick the bad guys out of the crowd." Even if you could be absolutely sure that the ID card correctly identified the person carrying it, that's no guarantee that said person hasn't been recruited to a new life of terrorism or crime. (Schneier points to Timothy McVeigh and the subway bombers in London as examples of those whose records would not have betrayed their intentions.) A perfectly effective identification program merely shifts who the terrorists choose to carry out an attack."

In another interesting development in January of 2008,

the State of Washington started issuing an "enhanced" driver's license as part of program developed by leaders in Washington and British Columbia to "... keep crossings between the United States and Canada convenient in the face of tightening regulations. The province is expecting an increased number of border crossings when its largest city, Vancouver, hosts the Winter Olympics in 2010. The state Legislature of Washington and U.S. Department of Homeland Security approved the enhanced driver's license.

"It absolutely is the first of its kind. ... We have received inquiries from many, many states about what it is that we've done and how it's working," said Brad Benfield, a spokesman for the Department of Licensing.

In a statement, Gregoire said the enhanced driver's license — as well as an enhanced state-issued identification card for those who don't drive — are "going to be a tremendous benefit and make travel faster and easier for our citizens."

Washington's enhanced license has a red border at the top and has several unique security features. It is equipped with radio-frequency identification technology aimed at allowing faster identification checks by border agents.

http://www.theolympian.com/news/story/335812.html

British Columbia introduced an enhanced driver's license the week of January 24, 2008.

In the search for better identity documentation, some have suggested Personal Hologram Imaging, in which the photograph of the person to whom identification papers are issued (passports, drivers' licenses, pilots' licenses, special airport speed-passes), are holograms that are difficult to fake because the equipment and technology would be classified, expensive, and highly proprietary.

Retinal Scan of the eye is a very reliable and unique identifier that could be embedded in various security systems. It's already being used by some high tech secured facilities, which you cannot enter without having an eye scan in addition to other security procedures.

Total Face Recognition is a developing technology that has been tested with varying degrees of reliability. Basically your face is imaged with a piece of equipment that "maps" out all your features. That imaging is entered into a database. You then step up to a reader (or your face can be captured by a special camera even at a distance without your knowledge) and matched against the image that has been recorded. If you match, then you gain access. This is being tested with the face prints of terrorists and criminals with the idea that you can catch these guys by having imaging cameras in appropriate places and scanning people entering or passing by until a person's face matches a criminal suspect.

Here is what one critic of this technology writes

"Facial identification is the fastest growing biometric technology today. According to many industry experts, it is also the most controversial of all biometrics. Despite their lingering questions regarding the practical usefulness of facial identification technology, law enforcement and military facial identification systems have been in place for several years without arousing too much controversy. According to industry insiders, this is because these applications have proven quite successful in carrying out specific objectives

and the public is often unaware of these uses. Although facial recognition technology has not been proven to be an accurate and effective way of identifying terrorists or wanted suspects, some of the proposed post-September 11 uses of the technology – such as in immigration and airport security – have been welcomed by the general public. Are we too eager to buy into a new technology without clearly evaluating its effectiveness and without weighing the potential harms involved with its use?"

"Are Privacy Rights of Citizens Being Eroded Wholesale?" by Angela Jarvis, http://forensic-evidence.com/site/ID/facialrecog.html

Incidentally, the forensic evidence web site is a fascinating place to study all kinds of different efforts to identify individuals including Lip Prints, Ear Prints, and Other Less Well-known Marks, Bite Mark Identification, Firearm and Toolmark Evidence, Handwriting and Forensic Document Examination, and the work of Dr. Itiel E. Dror (Ph.D. Harvard, 1994), a Senior Lecturer in the Department of Psychology at the University of Southampton, England, U.K. who does research in cognitive neuroscience. His special interest is in "… high-level cognitive phenomena, and his research encompasses visual-spatial abilities, mental imagery, decision making, and knowledge acquisition and expertise." Dr. Dror has demonstrated that even the best fingerprint evidence can be misread by experienced experts, thus leading to erroneous identifications.

Voiceprints can also be very effective security measures because, like fingerprints, the voice has a signature that is quite unique and distinct and, like fingerprints, it's still subject to misinterpretation.

Full body biometric is a way of recording a whole series of aspects of an individual including their heartbeat and other features and then using that image to match people.

Dental ID is a long used and proven way of matching jaw and dental features against records in a database. This technique is normally used to identify bodies where all the other identifying evidence has been destroyed or is unusable.

Smart Passport is a passport that has a series of not only money-like security characteristics but also has a digital data chip or transmitter that holds substantial and encrypted information about the bearer. This information could only be read by an official, government data reader, which should be a proprietary technology, used only by authorized officials.

A DNA ID is anything that uses the unique genetic print that separates one individual from another. DNA could be taken very unobtrusively with a mouth swab, for example, to match a person claiming to be you against a data bank of your DNA.

We recognize that all of these are high tech and almost science fiction-like ways of conducting security. This approach may be repulsive to some people and it does raise substantial civil liberties issues. On the other hand, we are living in a time when the traditional identification numbers and documents used in the United States are becoming extremely insecure if not obsolete. Some have argued that rather than protecting our civil liberties these easily stolen, duplicated, or forged documents are actually endangering our freedoms.

We highly recommend that the American Civil Liberties

Union, the Department of Justice and others need to join forces and explore more reliable and secure forms of identification for this twenty-first century. At the same time we must beef up our privacy laws so that citizens and consumers are protected from abuse of these new forms of documentation that presumably make it easier for government to monitor people.

New Airport Security Pass

On June 21, 2005 "passengers began lining up on Tuesday at Orlando International Airport to get their irises and fingerprints scanned in hopes of snagging one of 30,000 fast passes to be issued for airport security checkpoints. The airport and Verified Identity Pass, a company started by journalist and entrepreneur Steven Brill, are conducting the largest and first privately run test of biometric airport security measures in the United States.

For an annual membership fee of about $80, passengers who pass a federal background check and hold what the company is calling a Clear Card will be able to go through a special lane reserved for Clear users and will not be subject to the random secondary security checks encountered in the regular lanes.

"It's not skipping security," said Brigitte Goersch, director of Orlando Airport security. "It just takes away the unknown of how long the line is when you get there."

To get a Clear Card, passengers must provide biographical information on a form to be checked by the US Transportation Security Administration against federal terrorism and criminal databases, a process that takes about two weeks.

The TSA will make continuous security reviews of all members.

http://news.airwise.com/story/view/1119393864.html

The web site of the company http://www.verifiedidpass.com/ has further information on the process. According to the company;

Verified ID will not track or keep permanent records of where members travel and personal information provided as part of the screening process will not be shared or sold to any outside parties. Verified Identity Pass has created privacy policies that exceed the industry's best practices. These policies are available on the company's website at www.fly-clear.com.

One of the immediate questions that was brought up by students in our Electronic Democracy class was how secure these very detailed security files really are. Since they must be networked (so that information can be efficiently checked in a quick and timely manner), these records will, according to one expert we interviewed, become the prime target for computer hackers. The company holding this information therefore must have in place what we call "triple-super-whammy" security systems, surveillance, and a very complex encryption system. If they do not, it is very likely that a future news story will read, "Airport special access card files hacked!"

However, this should not happen because there is now heightened awareness of the risks of hacking and because the principals involved in developing this system are very reputable and include:

Steven Brill -- Steven Brill is the Founder and CEO of Verified Identity Pass, Inc. He has been a Newsweek columnist on all issues related to the aftermath of the September 11th attacks and a consultant to NBC on the same subject. He is the author of AFTER: How America Confronted The September 12th Era (Simon & Schuster 2003). Previously, he was Chairman and CEO, American Lawyer Media, L.P. and Founder, President, CEO and Editor-in-Chief of COURT TV (Courtroom Television Network).

Lockheed Martin -- One of the largest corporations in Orlando, Lockheed Martin employs about 130,000 people worldwide and is principally engaged in the research, design, development, manufacture and integration of advanced technology systems, products and services. Lockheed Martin Transportation and Security Solutions specializes in advanced aviation management, security and other mission-critical information technology solutions. Areas of focus include air traffic management; airport, physical and border security; and civil agency efforts involving advanced systems for managing sensitive information, such as census data capture, electronic records archiving, and communications network infrastructure programs.

<u>http://www.verifiedidpass.com/news_pr_062105.html</u>

Still, some of the banks such as CitiBank and other data companies that have been hacked in the recent past were also well known and yet had very weak and ineffective security protocols in place. Only time will tell if the computers and servers that hold and manage the Verified ID data base are sufficiently hardened and secure to protect them from attacks and theft.

A further criticism is that the cards are elitist and treat some people differently from others. Of course, anyone who has driven past the luxury hotel at $380 a night to pull into Motel 6 or anyone who has ever walked past the cushy First Class seats on most airplanes to get squeezed into the sardine can of discount class knows about elitism already!

Incidentally, Orlando International Airport gets a cut from the card company, so critics have said the airport may make regular security slow and nasty in order to encourage people to buy the premium card. If that happens and everyone flying through Orlando has a special pass, we assume the lines will once again become slow as molasses even with the $80 card!

Identity Theft Projections for 2008

The report, "2008 Identity Theft Outlook from the **Identity Theft Assistance Center**," is an interesting forward look at identity theft prospects. The Center reviewed major events related to identity theft in 2007 and from that extrapolated what it might mean for 2008.

The Identity Theft Assistance Center (www.identitytheftassistancecenter.com) is a nonprofit coalition of financial services companies "… united in our commitment to protect our customers from identity theft. As the leading provider of identity assistance services, ITAC protects all consumers through partnerships with law enforcement, education and identity management services."

Here is what the Center has reported as projections on ID theft:

• Criminals will continue to exploit new technologies to commit identity theft such as that committed by Gregory Kopiloff, 35 who was the first person indicted for using a peer-to-peer file sharing network, including LimeWire, to commit identity theft. Kopiloff allegedly used the software to steal tax returns, credit reports and bank statements, and then used that data to illegally purchase thousands of dollars' worth of products.

• Data security breaches will grow in importance as a business issue. Fallout from the TJX Companies, Inc. data breach, in which 45.6 million credit and debit card numbers were stolen from one of the company's systems, continued throughout 2007 a stark reminder of how information security can impact a company's bottom line. According to Ernst & Young's 10th annual Global Information Security Survey, 64 percent of the senior executives they surveyed said legal compliance was the top driver for security, followed by 58 percent who identified privacy and data protection as the No. 2 driver for security.

• The protection of personal information is an increasingly challenging political issue. United Kingdom Prime Minister Gordon Brown apologized to the nation following the loss of two CDs containing the personal and financial details of 25 million people. The incident was reminiscent of the data breach at the U.S. Department of Veterans Affairs, which exposed the personal information of 25 million and resulted in the call for public policy changes about how the government handles tax payer data. These types of losses will proliferate according to the Center.

• Identity thieves will continue to defy profiles. A twenty-something Philadelphia couple was arrested for stealing the identities of neighbors whose apartments they broke into. The Drexel University woman and her boyfriend, dubbed the "Bonnie and Clyde" of identity theft, used the proceeds to finance trips to Europe and Hawaii.

• Big busts and criminal penalties. An investigation by the Manhattan District Attorney's office and the U.S. Secret Service led to one of the year's biggest identity theft busts: 17 individuals and one business were indicted on charges of running a massive identity-theft and money-laundering operation that raked in more than $35 million over a four-year period. The individuals face up to 25 years each in prison. As law enforcement's capacity to investigate identity crime grows, so will the incidents of arrest and successful prosecutions.

Fromhttp://www.ad-hoc-news.de/index. html?section=CorporateNews&art_id=14890237&lang=en

The Center is also concerned about children's identity theft. There is fear that children's identity theft will also sharply accelerate in 2008 and beyond. In a report "Protect Your Kid's Future By Protecting ID: Child Identity Theft Rising, Government Agency Says" Leah Betancourt of WESH, Orlando reports that

"Turning 18 comes with new set of privileges -- the ability to vote, apply for a car loan or activate cell phone service. Imagine trying to do one of those things and being denied because someone stole your identity years earlier." Anne Wallace, president of the Identity Theft Assistance Center, said children are no greater or less a risk than adults. "It's

just that we don't expect it to happen to them," she said.
http://www.wesh.com/money/15121374/detail.html

One of the troubling possibilities that we have been investigating is that as the public becomes more aware of identity theft, potentially more people who never knew it existed and were not aware that it is a relatively easy crime may actually want to try ID theft as a profession. This hypothesis is derived from the fact that many illegal drug educators have come to realize that when drug prevention programs are taught in schools, many kids who have never heard of many of the drugs actually find out about them for the first time when the police officer brings the big "show-and-tell" board that has all the pills, marihuana, prescription drugs, mushrooms, crack, cocaine, methamphetamine and other "goodies" on display. One colleague who works with law enforcement has told us that "drug education" in schools may be just that – it teaches kids about all the substances that are out there for them to test.

Clearly the prospects for 2008 are not good for identity theft protection. With new technologies, more aggressive and impertinent criminals, and a predicted increase in children's identity theft, the need for better law enforcement and more personal and corporate vigilance is becoming urgent.

Conclusion

We have seen the past and present in the pages of this book. Now we have, like Ebenezer Scrooge in Dickens's A Christmas Carol, the future as well! Some of the futuristic security measures that may help make our identity more secure are still on the drawing board but others are in full field-testing deployment.

So what is a person to do?

First of all develop a TIA approach to life – **Total Identity Awareness**. This may seem awkward at first but it will soon become as natural as breathing. Tightly control all information about yourself. Don't give out any personal information – address, name, phone number, social security or credit card information, your resume or CV to people. Think of it as very valuable cash that can easily be stolen! Don't throw away letters or information that may contain identity property but instead tear up into tiny pieces, shred, or otherwise destroy this information.

If you subscribe to magazines and publications, dispose of them carefully and ALWAYS tear off the printed mailing information. This is a potential pathway to your identity. NEVER leave that magazine on the plane, lying around for others to take, or donate to the library without destroying that mailing information.

Don't leave anything in your car that has your name and other information and certainly DO NOT leave it lying face up so someone can just walk by and read it! We saw a hanger with dry cleaning in a truck at the grocery store parking lot, with the tag facing out – there was the name and address for all to see. If you must have some information in the car, lock up that registration or insurance form in the glove compartment. If your state requires you to have the insurance form or registration visible (a stupid idea in the first place), contact your legislators and work to have them change that law.

Check with your credit card company and find out what identity and credit card loss systems they have in place and push them to improve their standards. It is unbelievable that these companies are still mailing out all kinds of special neat offers for junk and airline bonus points but rarely if ever send out security related information and tips (or new services) with their monthly statements.

So, rule number one is to develop a defensive stance by making it hard for unauthorized people to get your information from you!

Second, we strongly recommend that you find a suitable identity theft services and use this as a "watchdog" of your identity. As we have said repeatedly in this book, in our lectures and training seminars, identity theft protection products provide a welcome peace of mind just like life or auto insurance. In the unfortunate case of a break in into your credit record, medical, educational, or general identity, these services provide some help and one even provides professional legal counsel to help in making it right again. We have referred to and provided contact information for some of these programs.

Third, keep up with the latest developments in security protection as well as theft. Use "safe computing" like safe sex! Have an Internet service provider (ISP) with a well-armored security system. Update your security software in your computer even though that is a relatively weak line of defense since new viruses and schemes are being launched on at least a daily basis. Don't go to high risk web sites, which are hard to define but try to read up on URL's (web addresses) that are mentioned in the media – our security consultant tells us that porn sites are notorious for spam and malware. NEVER download or execute anything sent to you unless you know what it is. Don't go to web sites to update your password and username – legitimate Internet firms and services normally don't ask you to do that – especially banks and credit card companies!

Fourth, get politically engaged. Contact your state legislators and encourage them to carefully examine state law to make sure that it is up to the highest standards for information security procedures. If your state does not have a CIO – Chief Information Officer – and a security division, get your governor to send a request in the next budget for a robust and credible Information Security and management division – It is well, well worth the cost. It's another layer in the homeland and personal defense system that we now need to put in place to protect ourselves and our institutions from serious attacks and losses.

Fifth, become politically active. Congress and the president MUST toughen up laws and reform the bureaucracy so that it is agile, aggressive, and modern in fighting identity theft. We need a national commitment to reforming the antiquated and hopelessly outdated social security card as a national ID number. We must resist the well-meaning but very dubious opposition by civil liberties groups such as the ACLU to developing a new, secure, reliable, and protected system of personal identification.

In the report "Future Trends in State Courts 2006: A Focus on Identity Theft, Social Security Numbers, and the Courts," our colleague José Dimas, Government Relations Associate, National Center for State Courts, has written a very interesting Future Trends Statement.

He "… examines the interest by federal policymakers to

tackle the problem of identity theft by restricting the display of Social Security numbers in public documents."

Did you know that one of the most egregious sources of good ID theft raw material are **court records** because Social Security numbers are public record in " ... probate files, land records, divorce documents, and other family-related court documents?"

This is a serious problem for consumers and persons who want their ID information protected. However, according to Mr. Dimas, it's also a serious problem for courts because they need Social Security numbers for procedures "... such as determining assets and income, identifying parties, and collecting fees, fines, and Restitution."

Three best practices for protecting SSNs, while still maintaining the traditional openness of courts have been discussed according to Dimas:

1) Creation of two sets of records, public and private;

2) Requirements that parties in cases be responsible for removing SSNs

3) Requirements that individuals use only the last four digits of SSNs.

Several states are already taking the lead in protecting litigants' Social Security numbers. Washington State is developing a procedure for sealing family-court records containing Social Security numbers and financial information. Vermont requires parties to remove these from court papers and Minnesota requires people in divorce cases to fill out a confidential information sheet, which is then kept separate from the official court record. South Dakota has also passed regulations removing the Social Security number from court records.

The lesson here is clearly that the Social Security number is the secret code to defending and protecting people's privacy and personal security.

The question now is whether a well-designed national identification card and system for verifying reliably the identity of every American citizen, resident, and guest in the United States is the best guarantee to protect us.

The British, as we reported in an earlier chapter, were moving towards a national ID card. Then a careless bureaucrat lost the records of almost half of all Brits by shipping the data via courier. The British government suddenly realized that a national identity number is worthless if the government is going to compromise it. And in fact, having a national Id number may put people at more risk under these circumstances.

The bottom line is that we are living in a stressful and trying period of history. The economy, terrorism, rising fuel prices, sex crimes, global warming, a big national debt, job security, a Social Security system that needs repair, the rising costs of Medicare and Medicaid (and general health care) are all things about which we as individuals can do very little! However, smart identity security management IS something we can control and we can materially improve our personal tranquility and happiness by being identity smart.

This book has given you a "cold shower" on identity threats and solutions. We also hope that after an initial shock, fear, and awe at the extensiveness and cleverness of identity criminals, you are now well prepared to engage in better identity self defense!

If we all exercise best practice and are reasonably prudent, we can better protect our identity and financial security.

We can also exercise our civic right to press state and federal leaders to substantially strengthen the policies and enforcement mechanisms that will make us personally and our nation a safer place in the future.

We hope that this book has been informative and that your personal identity and that of your family members, and customers, if you have any, will be more secure as a result. We have added several appendices with some specific information that you may want to find quickly.

WHAT TO DO IF YOUR IDENTITY IS STOLEN
(General Resource Information for Individuals)

• File a written police report immediately and maintain a copy for your records. You may need it later to validate claims to creditors.

• Depending on the circumstances, you may want to contact your insurance company.

• Take steps to formally notify, in writing, those whose records and personal information may have been compromised, i.e. employees, customers, family, etc.

• Contact the fraud departments of each of the three major credit bureaus:

EQUIFAX: 800-525-6285, P.O. Box 740241, Atlanta, GA 30374-0241, www.equifax.com

EXPERIAN: 888-397-3742, P.O. Box 9532, Allen, TX 75013, www.experian.com

TRANS UNION: 800-680-7289, Fraud Victim Assistance Division, P.O. Box 6790, Fullerton, CA 92834-6790, www.tuc.com

Ask them to place a fraud alert in your file as well as a victim statement. This is a signal to creditors to contact you before any changes can be made to your accounts.

• Close any accounts that have been tampered with or opened fraudulently. (These include credit card accounts, banks and other lenders, phone and utility companies, and other service providers. Any new accounts opened later should have new PINs and passwords.)

• File a complaint with the Federal Trade Commission (FTC) Identity Theft Hotline 877-438-4338 or go to www.consumer.gov/idtheft. Obtain and complete the ID Theft affidavit, keep a copy for your records. Your FTC complaint will be entered into a secure consumer fraud database (Identity Theft Clearinghouse), accessible only to law enforcement agencies for use in pursuing criminal investigations.

• For information in Spanish for victims of ID Theft, refer to www.privacyrights.org/spanish/fs17(a)sp.htm

Additional agencies/organizations to contact include but are not limited to:

UNITED STATES POSTAL INSPECTOR:
Contact your local post office for the phone number of the nearest postal inspection service or check the postal service website: www.usps.gov/websites/depart/inspect

FEDERAL BUREAU OF INVESTIGATION:
Local field offices are listed in the blue pages of your telephone directory. You can also access the FBI's website at www.fbi.gov

BETTER BUSINESS BUREAU: Contact your nearest BBB office to check the reputation of a company and/or if you have a problem resolving fraudulent charges. To locate a BBB online, go to www.bbb.org

SOCIAL SECURITY:
If your Social Security number is being misused, contact the social security hotline 800-269-0271, P.O. Box 17768, Baltimore, MD 21235 www.ssa.gov

CHEX SYSTEMS, INC.:
1-800-428-9623; www.chexhelp.com Fax: 602-659-2197 Chex Systems, Inc. Attn: Consumer Relations 7805 Hudson Road, Suite 100 Woodbury, MN 55125

TELECHECK:
1-800-710-9898 or 927-0188

Answers.com, http://www.answers.com/topic/business-ethics?cat=biz-fin

The Anti-Phishing Working Group, http://www.antiphishing.org/

Berinato, Scott, "The future of security," December 30, 2003, http://www.computerworld.com/printthis/2003/0,4814,88646,00.html

Betancourt, Leah, "Protect Your Kid's Future By Protecting ID Child Identity Theft **Rising, Government Agency Says**," http://www.wesh.com/money/15121374/detail.html

Blankenhorn, Dana, "Worried about your medFICO score" Column, December 12th, 2007, http://healthcare.zdnet.com/?p=570

Boucher, Tim. "Erasing Personal History," http://www.timboucher.com/journal/2006/12/09/erasing-personal-history/

Broder, Betsy, "Identity Protection Strategies," http://www.bankinfosecurity.com/podcasts.php?podcastID=71

Canadian Bankers Association, "Identity Theft: An Old Problem Needing a New Approach"; "PhoneBusters Identity Theft Statistics", RCMP-CCB Ottawa; http://www.publicsafety.gc.ca/prg/le/bs/report-en.asp#_ftn19

Carr, Jim, "Colombian pleads guilty to internet-based ID theft scam," SC magazine on Line, http://www.scmagazineus.com/Colombian-pleads-guilty-to-internet-based-ID-theft-scam/article/104161/

"Change Your Identity," http://www.ariza-research.com/new-id/

Coates, James, "Wi-Fi hackers find routes easily; path tough to block," Chicago Tribune, reported in the Los Angeles Times, July 10, 2005.

"The Coming Pandemic," CIO Magazine, May 15, 2006.

Compliance Headquarters, http://www.complianceheadquarters.com

Consumer Federation of America, http://forum.creditcourt.com/discus/messages/10/624.html

Consumeraffairs.com, "Your Right to Be Left Alone, and How You Can Protect It," Jan. 20, 2008 http://www.consumeraffairs.com

Dimitrov, Vladimir and Kalevi Kopra, "Dynamics of Human Identity," http://www.zulenet.com/VladimirDimitrov/pages/identity.html

"The doctor will see your credit now," http://redtape.msnbc.com/2008/01/the-doctor-wi-1.html#posts

Edwards, Mark, "Freedom from Personal History: A Toltec View." http://www.lightworks.com/monthlyAspectarian/2004/March/feature2.htm

"Ex-inmate frustrated by freedom," Man who served time for TV theft can't get identity," Charleston Post and Courier

"The Fair and Accurate Transactions Act," NFIB, http://www.nfib.com

FTC – "Take Charge: Fighting Back Against Identity Theft," http://www.ftc.gov/bcp/edu/pubs/consumer/idtheft/idt04.shtm

Federal Trade Commission, "How to Protect Kids' Privacy Online", http://www.ftc.gov/bcp/menus/consumer/data/child.shtm.

Federal Trade Commission, ID Theft laws, http://www.consumer.gov/idtheft/federallaws.html#criminalstate

Felten, Edward W., " Pharming," Freedom to Tinker, http://www.freedom-to-tinker.com/?p=781

References

Fountain, Henry, "Worry. But Don't Stress Out," The New York Times, June 26, 2005, Section 4, p. 1.

Garretson, Cara, "Taming the ever-evolving phish risk," http://www.network-world.com/news/2005/013105phishing.html

Greek, Dinah, "Watch what you say online," http://www.infomaticsonline.co.uk/vnunet/news/2122773/watch-say-online

Harwood, Matthew, "British Government Loses Private Data of 7.5 Million Families," Security Management, 11/20/2007, http://www.securitymanagement.com/print/2821

Healey, John, "The false promise of Real ID: Homeland Security's compromises make an ineffective law somewhat less damaging," January 22, 2008, the Los Angeles Times.

Hill, Christian, "State rolls out enhanced driver's license," The Olympian, Jan 23, 2008, http://www.theolympian.com/news/story/335812.html

HIPPA, http://www.hhs.gov/ocr/hipaa

The Houston Chronicle, "Interview with Chertoff", http://www.chron.com/disp/story.mpl/editorial/5454204.html

Identity Theft - Facts and Figures, National Criminal Justice References Service, http://www.ncjrs.gov/spotlight/identity_theft/facts.html

"2008 Identity Theft Outlook from the Identity Theft Assistance Center,"http://www.ad-hoc-news.de/index.html?section=CorporateNews&art_id=14890237&lang=en

"IRS Warns Taxpayers of New E-mail Scams," Internal Revenue Service, http://www.irs.gov/newsroom/article/0,,id=170894,00.html

Jaffe, Huck, "Stupid Investment of the Week: Identity-theft insurance isn't even worth its small price," MarketWatch, Dec. 5, 2006,

Jarvis, Angela, "Are Privacy Rights of Citizens Being Eroded Wholesale?" http://forensic-evidence.com/site/ID/facialrecog.html

Jordan, Erin, Iowa researcher probes 'Blissful Ignorance Effect,' The Des Moines Register, February 1, 2008.

Kane, Nancy, "Medical Bad Debt – A Growing Public Health Crisis," House Ways and Means Committee, US Congress. http://waysandmeans.house.gov/hearings.asp?formmode=view&id=1686

Krause, Jason, "Stolen Lives," March 2006, ABA Journal, http://www.saloncredit.com/idtheft/stolen_lives_aba_journal.pdf

Labaton, Stephen, "An Army of Soulless 1's and 0's," The New York Times, June 24, 2005

Leyden, John, "Spyware fears prompt changing net habits," http://www.theregister.com/2005/07/07/spyware_survey_pew/

"Life is Good Settles Security Charges with FTC," The Boston Business Journal, Thursday, January 17, 2008.

Mallia, Joseph. "Cops: Carle Place Worker nabbed in ID Theft," Newsday, Jan 15, 2008.

Mark, Roy, "Congress Closer to National ID Theft Law," http://www.internetnews.com/security/article.php/3520586

Marks, Paul, "Attempted Cyber-heist raises keylogging fears," http://www.newscientist.com/channel/info-tech/electronic-threats/dn7168

Matthew Cox Case, United States Attorney David E. Nahmias Northern District of Georgia http://www.usdoj.gov/usao/gan/

McLellan,Vin, "CYBER CORPS' FAILING GRADES. Federal officials are revamping the infosec training program to resolve critical job placement problems," http://infosecuritymag.techtarget.com/2003/jun/cybercorps.shtml

"Medical Identity Theft on the Rise," http://www.safetysend.com/Medical-Identity-Theft.htm

Moodley-Isaacs, Neesa, "New Bill to curtail identity fraud," January 26, 2008, http://www.persfin.co.za/index.php?fArticleId=4224618&fSectionId=592&fSetId=300

"Orlando Airport to Eyeball Vetted Passengers," Airwise News, Feb. 16, 2008, http://news.airwise.com/story/view/1119393864.html

"Orlando International Airport and CLEAR TM Open Enrollment for Registered Traveler Program," http://www.verifiedidpass.com/news_pr_062105.html

"New Hawaii Identity Theft Laws," http://hawaii.gov/dcca/quicklinks/id_theft_info/laws/ID_Theft_Info_For_Businesses

Office of the Privacy Commissioner of Canada, http://www.privcom.gc.ca/aboutUs/index_e.asp

"Online Apparel Retailer Settles FTC Charges that it Failed to Safeguard Consumers' Sensitive Information in violation of Federal Law," http://www.ftc.gov/opa/2008/01/lig.shtm

"Ontario Becomes First Canadian Jurisdiction With Credit Alert Legislation," Ontario Ministry of Government and Consumer Services, http://www.newswire.ca/en/releases/archive/January2008/23/c3473.html

Pharming.org, http://www.pharming.org/index.jsp

Popken, Ben, Ed.,"TSA Traveler Website Exposed Private Citizens To Risk of ID Theft." The Consumerist, Jan 15, 2008.

Privacy Rights Clearing House, http://www.privacyrights.org/fs/fs17-it.htm

"The Red Flag Rule," http://www.ftc.gov/os/2007/10/r611019redflagsfrn.pdf

"Report on Identity Theft," Public Safety Canada, http://www.publicsafety.gc.ca/prg/le/bs/report-en.asp

"Scam Wars: Phishing Kits Exploit Customers," http://www.pcworld.com/businesscenter/article/141688/scam_wars_phishing_kits_exploit_customers.html

Scamwatch.gov, "About the Australasian Consumer Fraud Taskforce," http://www.scamwatch.gov.au/content/index.phtml/itemId/694357

Schenk, Robert, "Rational Ignorance," http://ingrimayne.com/econ/LogicOfChoice/RatIgnorance.html

Science for All Americans Online, "The Human Organism," http://www.project2061.org/publications/sfaa/online/chap6.htm

"Senior Citizens Vulnerable To ID Theft Scams: New E-Mail Circulating Poses As IRS," http:www.local10.com

References

"Senator Feinstein Holds Hearing on Identity Theft," http://feinstein.senate.gov/releases00/identity_theft_bill_hearing.html

Silverston, Len, "National Intelligence and the Integration Gap: Terrorism: A Call for Data Integration," DM Direct Newsletter, November 16, 2001.

Sherburne Co. Sheriff, "Storage Lockers Burglarized," The Sherburne County **Minnesota Sheriff's Department,** http://www.co.sherburne.mn.us/sheriff/news/2002/PR111402.htm

Singel, Ryan,"Zombie Computer Army Targets Bank Account Passwords," http://blog.wired.com/27bstroke6/2008/01/zombie-computer.html

Society for Human Resource managers, "Identity Theft Awareness," Michigan **Council 25 of AFSCME,** http://www.shrm.org 5/2/05

"Spear phishing: Highly targeted scams," http://www.microsoft.com/protect/yourself/phishing/spear.mspx

Spychips.com, "VERICHIP RFID IMPLANT HACKED! Will Security Problems **Quash IPO Plans for Controversial Company?"** http://www.spychips.com/press-releases/verichip-hacked.html

Vamosi, Robert, ed., "Alarm over pharming attacks: identity theft made even easier," http://reviews.cnet.com/4520-3513_7-5670780-1.html)

"Virus writer exploits London bomb blast," July 11, 2005, http://www.optusnet.com.au

The White House, "Fact Sheet: The President's Identity Theft Task Force" http://www.whitehouse.gov/news/releases/2006/05/20060510-6.html

Shoop, Tom, "ID Theft Gets Real," blog entry January 16, 2008, http://blogs.gov-exec.com/fedblog/2008/01/id_theft_gets_real.php

http://www.inrich.com/cva/ric/news.apx.-content-articles-RTD-2008-01-15-0194.html

"U.S. Announces What Is Believed The Largest Identity Theft Case In American History; Losses Are In The Millions," U.S. Department of Justice, http://www.usdoj.gov/criminal/cybercrime/cummingsIndict.htm

Social Security Administration, "Information About Your Statement," www.ssa.gov/mystatement.

"Two Defendants Sentenced in Health Care Fraud", HIPAA, and "Identity Theft Conspiracy, the Ferrer & Machado Case", Southern District of Florida - Press Release http://www.usdoj.gov/usao/fls/PressReleases/070503-01.html

US population clock. http://www.census.gov/main/www/popclock.html

Yuille, Brigitte, "How your child's stolen identity can be used," http://www.bank-rate.com/

Index